WITH THE DIGITAL EVOLUTION, underwater photography has never been easier. But simply finding that rare fish or using a nude model is not a guarantee for a good underwater picture. The mastering of photographic craftsmanship is an essential requirement for producing good work.

This book takes you from the basics, channels your creativity to greater heights and guides you to produce some of the most beautiful pictures of the sea. It will also help you to learn the art form of photography and master the vocabulary of digital imaging. Above all this book will open your eyes to the enjoyment of digital underwater photography increasing the fun factor of your diving.

Dive Safe, Shoot Well!

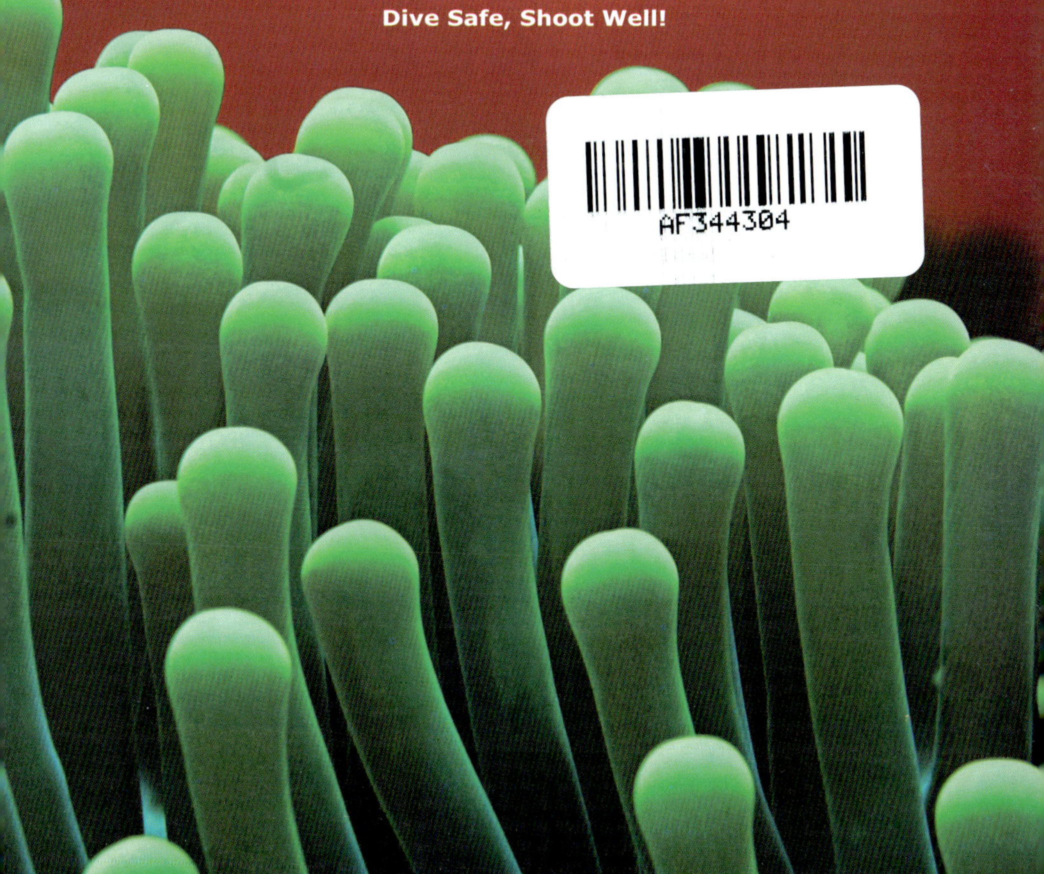

The MEGA PIXEL RACE

While we embraced the advancement of digital technology, camera manufacturers are mega money crazy – they are producing new models faster than they can change their underwear! New models are introduced every month with little increment in features that are mostly unnecessary. DON'T get caught up with the newer and bigger megapixel (MP) contest!

Invest in the best available system that you can afford – the longer you wait, the more photo opportunities you miss. If you are shooting with a five to eight megapixel camera, you are already capable of producing high quality images. The epitome of wildlife photography comeptitions – the BBC Wildlife Photographer of Year Competition was won by Doug Perrine in 2004 with an image captured with a 6 MP SLR launched into the market in 2002!

With some post editing refinement and a good printer, you will be able to produce saleable 20" x 24" fine art photographic prints from a 5 MP camera. Print quality is really subjective that are attributed to many factors that are more important than pixels; camera and lens quality, post editing, printer quality, colour profiling and viewing distance. Remember the most important element in making a good picture, is you, your eyes behind the camera.

HOW TO USE THIS GUIDE

Digital cameras are making waves into the future of underwater imaging. This guide offers aspiring photographers step by step comprehensive instructions to learning the art of digital underwater photography and most importantly how to capture successful images. Consequently, some of the material presented here may at times be more relevant to one user group than another. Both beginners and advanced digital shooters will benefit from using this guide. As you browse you will quickly identify answers to your questions and with practice you will progressively achieve award winning images.

For new shooters you may wish to first quickly peruse from cover to cover for an overview of underwater digital imaging. However this guide is structured like a Bible of digital photography, you can refer for knowledge of specific interest from designated modules or pick up step by step instructions from the 'How to' sections. Experienced shooters may choose to fast track the learning process through the Classic MASTERPIECES and knowledge review section in Module Five. For easy referencing, each module is colour coded.

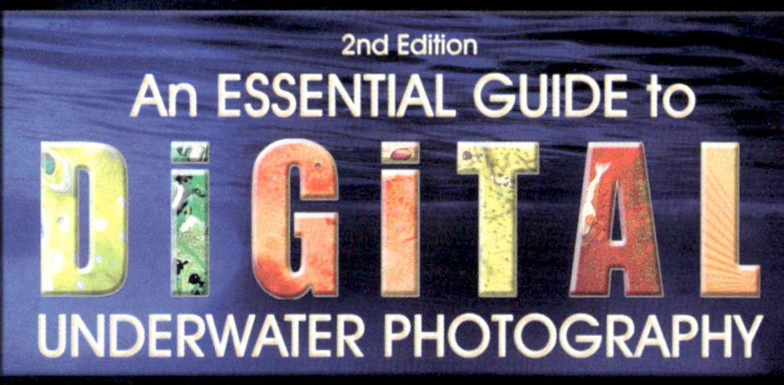

Michael AW

with **Mathieu Meur**

This guide DOES not replace the manuals from your camera and housing manufacturers. Use Module One as an addendum to know your equipment better and shooting underwater. In Module Two and Three we reveal in simple steps how to create great underwater pictures. In Module Four, you will learn to be a digital darkroom technician and in Module Five, you can practise by recreating masterpieces esf underwater imagery.

Most importantly, diving is meant to be fun, and underwater photography is rewarding allowing you to bring back your experience to share with family and friends. If you strive to win a few awards or sell a few images along the way, all the more rewarding.

CONTENTS

HOW to do that?

CHECKLIST:

Published by
OceanNEnvironment
Member of Environment Australia
www.OceanNEnvironment.com : www.michaelaw.com
Email: michael@oneocean.com
PO Box 2138, Carlingford, NSW 2118, Australia

Design by Michael AW
Editor: Alison Redhead / Christopher Lee
Illustrations: Alison Redhead / Michael AW
Art Director: John Thet

www.michaelaw.com Copyright OceanNEnvironment 2004 / 2ND EDITION - 2006
Michael AW/ Mathieu Meur, National Library of Australia Cataloguing-Publication Entry
An Essential Guide to Digital Underwater Photography ISBN: 1 876381 05 1

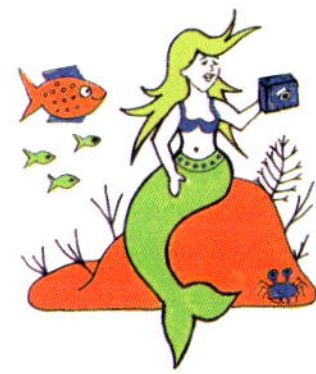

Getting Started

1. Buy the Best you can afford – consider the budget you have at your disposal – get the best. This will ensure that you can grow with your system, and possibly a system that can grow with you – ideally pick a system that offers the possibility to expand – adding strobes, filters, lenses.

2. Diving experience – underwater photography demands a great deal of concentration and diving skill. Essentially you must be comfortable and dexterous in the water. You must be able to hover like a fish, make quick judgements and be proficient in scuba safety skills. We recommend that you have made 50 leisure dives (that is not counting training dives) before trying to shoot underwater. Avoid stirring up the ocean and using corals and sponges as brakes! Holding on to them is unacceptable – it makes you a very bad photographer. Perfect buoyancy is an absolute necessity not only for the sake of your pictures but also for the well being of the reef. NO photograph is worth damaging a reef, or molesting a sea creature. A consequence of having good buoyancy control is lower air consumption thereby maximizing shooting time. There is no substitute for underwater time, you will need the experience to dive and shoot safely. Never let the distractions of Photography compromise diving safety.

3. The Golden Rule – Get Close

Get close, get rid of the water. Getting close reduces the column of water between you and your subject, reducing potential backscatter, resulting in clearer shots, allowing your subject to occupy a greater portion of the frame. Move with purpose, avoid jerky movements. Be relaxed, and be in control of your movements then the reef will relax too. Fishes are more approachable if you move slowly patiently and in control. It goes without saying that you need to be fairly stable to avoid blurred images.

Remember: if your picture is not good enough, you are not close enough.

4. Knowledge RULES – an in-depth knowledge of your subject is the key to successful images. Knowing marine habitats, who lives where, when they eat and where they sleep and how animals react to your presence. A good understanding of animal behaviour and the ability to predict their movement greatly increases your chance of success.

5. Remember ASS – Assess water integrity, Assess flash fire above and below, Assess that media is installed and all controls are assessable. Shoot from left, from right, from bottom – vary camera angles, Shoot with bracketing – plus one stop, minus one stop. Shoot as much as possible – digital media is cheap. Save images in tiff file, save enhanced images, save originals and back up on CD.

Module ONE
Digital Essentials

1/1 Digital Evolution

Until the advent of digital, the most frustrating thing for a new underwater photographer was the preposterously low success rate. It was not uncommon for a beginner to return with his first 10 rolls of film only to find 90% of the pictures either over or underexposed. The successful 10% were at best images of perhaps half a fish tail or out of focus pictures of their buddy. Underwater photography was but a cruel joke for most. Digital photography provided sudden advantages over traditional film for the underwater photographer.

Advantages:

1. Immediate review of images. Underexposed? Shoot again and vary the composition, then shoot another 10, if you need to.
2. By using a large storage media such as a 1GB or 4GB Compact flash card, you will never run out of film.
3. Another result of digital is the tremendous saving on consumables and incidentals – there will be no need to buy film, and pay for processing loads of shots which have a high probability of ending up in the bin.
4. Since it is not necessary to spend any money on consumables, you can afford to be trigger happy, shoot more to hone your skills without risking spending a small fortune. The learning curve can be as steep as you like without making a hole in your wallet.
5. Another advantage of digital technology is the tremendous flexibility that this medium can afford. Whether at home or while on holidays, you can email pictures to your friends and family to share, or post them on the web, review them on your computer and create slideshows.

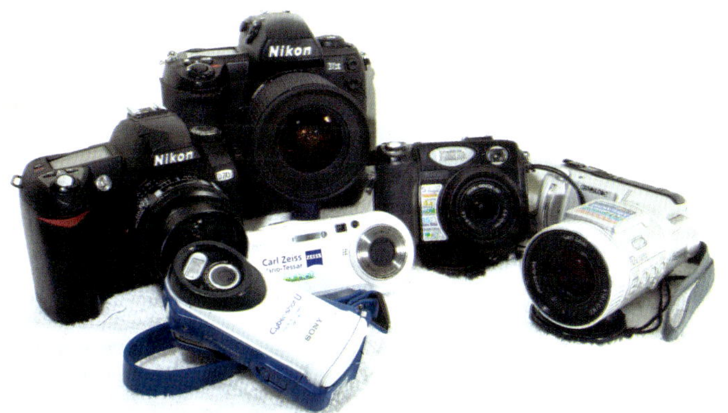

Consumer, Prosumer and DSLR digital cameras.

Understanding Digital Photographic Language

In order to get the most out of your digital camera, it is important to first understand a few technical terms.

Aperture: The aperture can be thought of like the iris of the eye. The larger the aperture, the more light gets into the camera, and vice-versa. Aperture values are typically represented in f-stops (e.g. f/2.0, f/2.8, f/4, f/5.6 etc.). The greater the number, the smaller the aperture is. The aperture you set on your camera also has an impact on the depth-of-field. If all other parameters are constant, the smaller the aperture, the greater the depth-of-field is and vice versa.

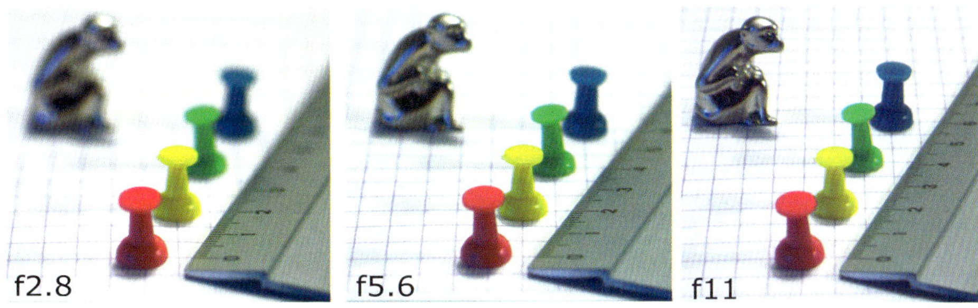

Depth-of-Field (DOF): Depth-of-field refers to the area of the photograph in front and behind the main focus point which appears sharp. A large depth-of-field means a greater portion of the picture is in focus. Conversely, in order to emphasise a certain feature or area of the picture, you may use a shallower depth-of-field, which will result in a blurred background.

Shutter speed: The shutter speed is the length of time that the camera allows light (the image you are capturing) to reach the sensor. Shutter speed is normally indicated in seconds (e.g. 2s, 1/125s, etc.). Long shutter speeds mean more light is allowed to reach the sensor, which is desirable in low light conditions, but may result in camera shake (blurred picture). Conversely, faster shutter speeds allow the photographer to freeze the action, but may result in dark pictures if there is not enough light.

Sensor: The sensor (commonly referred to as a CCD or CMOS in digital cameras) is the electronic chip which records light falling on it, in the digital camera. It is the device which actually captures the picture. This chip is made of millions of tiny electronic receptors which are sensitive to light. The camera reads the "image" formed on these components for further processing. CCDs use a unique process to create the aptitude to transport electrons across the chip without distortion. This process leads to very high-quality sensors in terms of fidelity and light sensitivity. CMOS chips, on the other hand, use an old-fashioned manufacturing process to create the chip, which is the same process used to make most microprocessors. Because of the differing manufacturing processes, there are notable differences between CCD and CMOS sensors:

- CCD sensors create high-quality, low-noise images. CMOS sensors, traditionally, are more susceptible to noise.
- CMOS traditionally consumes little power.
- CCDs use a process that consumes lots of power. However with the use of Lithium-Ion or Nickel-Metal Hydride batteries, this is not a problem with digital cameras using a CCD sensor.
- CMOS chips can be fabricated on just about any standard silicon production line, so they tend to be extremely inexpensive compared to CCD sensors.
- CCD sensors have been mass-produced for a longer period of time for digital imaging, so they are more mature.

Based on these differences, CCDs tend to be used in cameras that focus on high-quality images with lots of pixels and excellent light sensitivity. CMOS sensors traditionally have lower quality, lower resolution and lower sensitivity. As such CMOS cameras are usually less expensive. New CMOS chips used in some DSLR's heralds new advances in this technology and the jury is still out on which technology will emerge dominant.

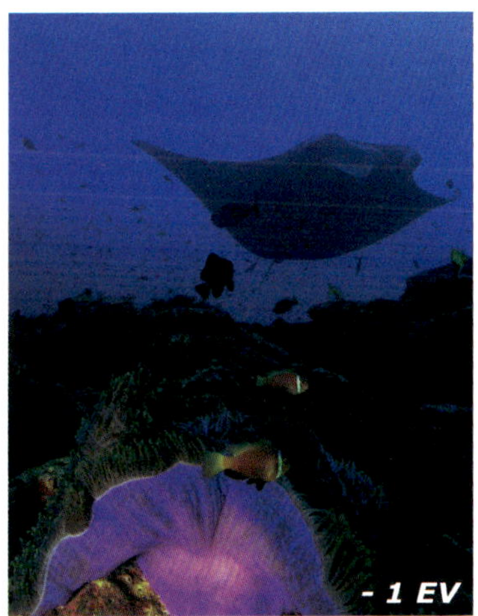

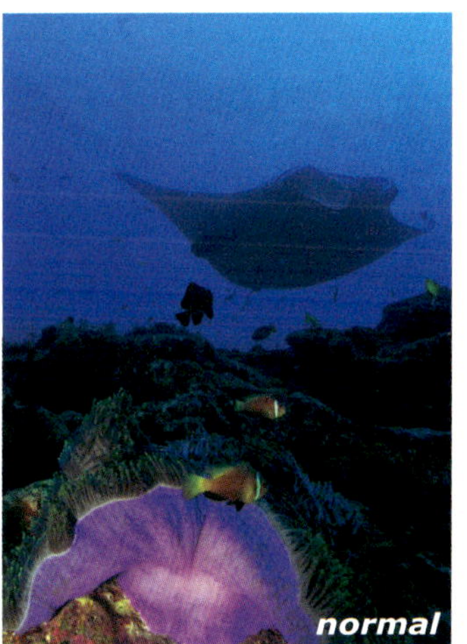

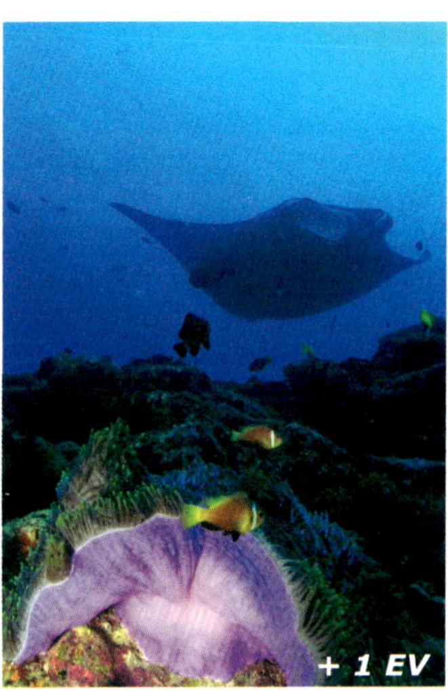

Exposure Value (EV): The exposure value is the actual exposure of the digital camera's sensor to light when taking a photograph. This is the combination of the sensitivity of the sensor (ISO number), aperture and shutter speed. Exposure value compensation (+/- button on the camera) lets you increase or decrease the exposure.

Sensitivity (ISO number): This term is used as an analogy to traditional film camera systems. In digital photography, the image recorded is based on an electric current that is proportional to the amount of light that is received by the sensor. This current is very small and needs to be amplified. Consequently, in a similar fashion to what is the case in traditional film photography, higher ISO numbers in digital cameras also result in visible grain, called noise.

White Balance: The white balance is a name given to a system of colour correction to deal with differing lighting conditions. For example, a white slate shot underwater will appear bluish or greenish. White balance can correct this to make the slate appear white.

Resolution: The resolution describes the number of light-sensitive receptors in the digital camera. This number dictates the maximum size in pixels of the images generated by the digital camera (e.g. 2560 pixels x 1920 pixels). What is confusing is that there are sometimes two numbers given by the manufacturers (e.g. 3.3 megapixels, 3.1 effective). This means that the camera is fitted with 3.3 million receptors, but the information provided only by 3.1 million of these receptors is used to form the final pictures. The remaining 200,000 receptors are used for other purposes (for example, some are "painted" black to give to the camera a reference as to what black is).

For example, we have tested the Sony Cyber Shot 50 (2.1 million pixel camera) with a Carl Zeiss lens and a Sony Cyber shot P1 (3.4 million pixel camera). Set both to shoot at 1600 x 1200, the Sony Cyber Shot 50 produced a better quality picture because of the more expensive lens system. So what is the difference between a 3MP and a 2MP camera? Simple: divide the pixel count by 200 - assuming that you are printing a picture at 200 dpi (dots per inch), which is the lowest recommended for a printed photograph. For a 3MP camera, the pixel count is 2048 x 1536 which will produce a good 8" x 10" print (about 20cm x 25cm). For a 2MP camera, the pixel count is 1600 x 1200 the final picture size printed at 200 dpi will only yield a 6" x 8" print (about 15cm x 20cm). Unless you have a super fast camera with lots of buffer memory, the higher the resolution, the longer the recording time, i.e. the longer you have to wait to take the next picture. Thus, it is a trade-off between quality and speed you have to consider here.

Image Compression: Joint Photographic Experts Group (JPEG) – digital cameras typically store images as a jpeg file, the most common compression file format for pictures. A good camera will let you adjust the compression level – basic, normal, fine or superfine and some will even let you store lossless RAW or uncompressed Tiff, a professional grade file most commonly used in publishing.

Shutter lag: This term refers to the delay that occurs between the moment the photographer presses the shutter release button, and the moment the picture is actually taken. A long shutter lag has been typical of consumer digital cameras. High end digital cameras typically have no or almost no shutter lag. Acceptable shutter lag at this point for a camera should be faster than 1/10th second.

Important NOTE: ***Higher resolution does not mean better quality*** – it just means that you can make a larger picture. Aside from the photographer's skill, the quality of a shot depends mostly on the quality of the optics, the quality of the sensor, and the image-processing chip used by the camera. This means that an 8MP camera with average optics and sensor could yield pictures which are inferior in quality to those produced by a 5MP camera with superior optics, and better sensor and imaging chip. The resolution itself is only a count of how many dots of light are recorded by the sensor.

Digital Film – Storage media

Instead of film most digital cameras store images on a range of memory cards – the most common being Smart Media and Compact Flash; the latter type being more correctly known as CompactFlash Association (CFA) certified Type I and Type II memory cards. Type II is identical in size to Type I except for its thickness, which is 2 mm greater, providing for more memory to be added. Generally the most popular among serious shooters are the Microdrives by IBM and Hitachi. With a capacity of up to 4GB: they are the most cost effective 'digital film'. SONY has its own proprietary system – the Memory Stick.

As chip prices have fallen and the market expanded the cost has fallen dramatically while capacity has risen. Typically, storage media come in 8MB, 16MB, 32MB, 64MB, 128MB, 256MB, 512MB to 4GB. The principal advantage of digital cameras is that if you don't like the picture, you can simply delete them right there and then and re-shoot. Though most housings allow you to delete unwanted pictures, underwater time is precious, so we suggest that you use a bigger memory card like a 256MB or a 1GB to shoot to your heart's content and delete the unwanted images after the dive.

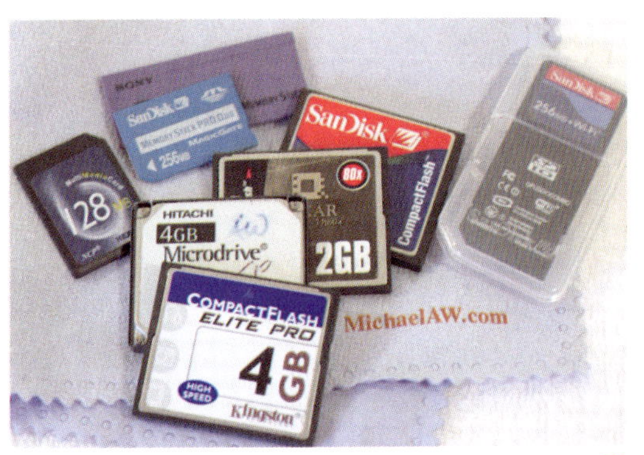

Image Capacity - Storage media

**JPEG calculated @ highest setting. Figures are estimate; size of image varies.*

CARD SIZE	1 GB		2 GB		4 GB	
RESOLUTION / File type	JPEG	RAW	JPEG	RAW	JPEG	RAW
4MP (2288x1712)	384	210	768	420	1536	840
6MP (3008x2012)	300	102	600	205	1200	411
8MP (3264x2448)	276	60	552	120	1105	240
12MP (4288x2848)	227	50	455	101	910	203

Focal Length and Effective Focal Length (EFL): In film photography, the focal length measures the angle or field of view of a particular lens. The smaller the figure (e.g. 12mm or 16mm), the wider the field of view is and the smaller the subject will appear on the picture. Conversely, the greater the figure (e.g. 300mm), the narrower the field of view is and the larger it will appear on the photo. The focal length also influences the appearance of the subjects on the picture. Wider lenses tend to distort the picture, creating a noticeable curvature at the perimeter of the image. This is normally not a problem underwater, as there are few straight lines.

In digital cameras, the sensor is typically smaller than the traditional 35mm film frame (24mmX36mm). Therefore, the sensor "sees" a smaller portion of the picture than what a traditional camera would see. Consequently, the image appears to have been taken with a different lens having a longer (greater number) focal length. In actual fact, the most accurate way to describe this would be "field-of-view crop", since the image seen by the lens is the same, but the sensor only gets to record the centre portion of this image.

When a Nikkor 60mm macro lens is used with a Nikon D100 or Fuji S2 DSLR, the 1.6 multiplier seemingly gives a focal length of 96mm. Because of the smaller sensor format of DSLRs, the 60mm lens has a narrower angle of view than when it is used on a 35mm film camera – a smaller portion of the image circle projected by the lens is used, therefore it is a 'crop' on the imaging area. The image remains the same size at the film plane for the 60mm lens and subject distance – it is in no way magnified. It does, however, take up a larger proportion of the (smaller) frame and so it is easy to see why it is sometimes referred to as a magnifying effect. This is also why a macro lens appears so much more powerful in digital - the field or angle-of-view has been reduced. This is great for macro photography as the net result is much bigger.

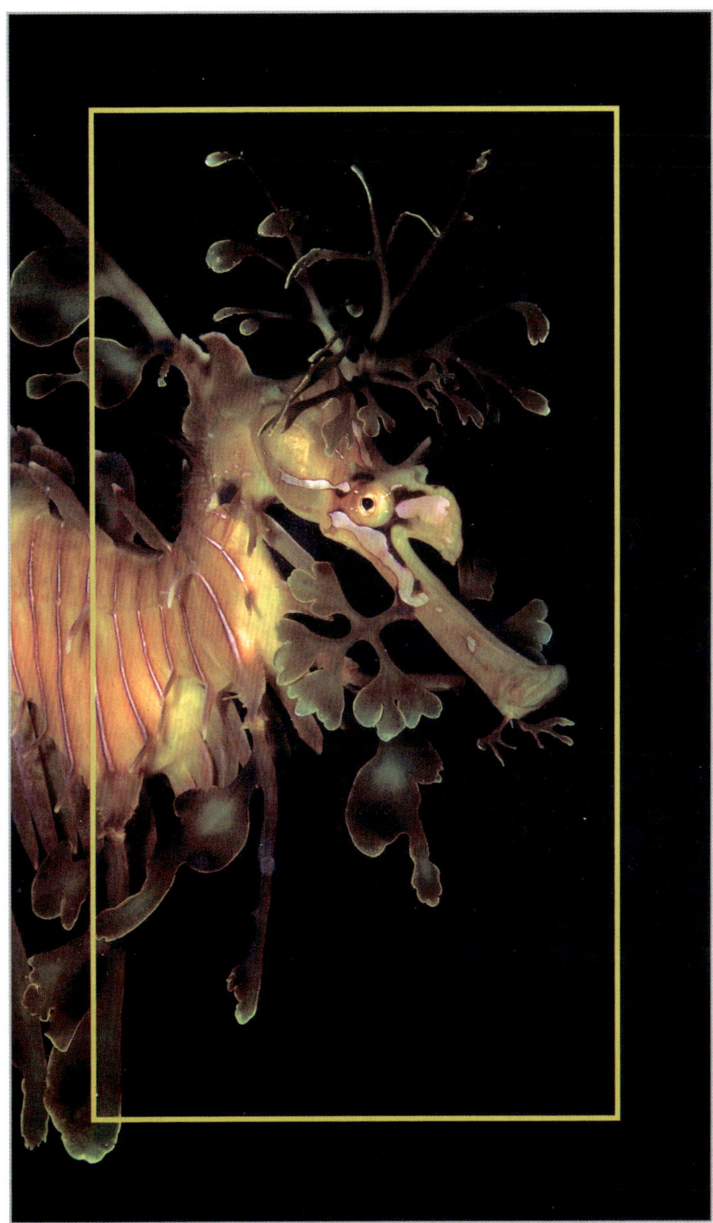

The full frame image shows the capture area taken with a 35mm film camera or a full-frame digital SLR using a 60mm macro lens. The inner green frame shows what a digital SLR with a 1.6X magnification factor will capture. It is similar to 'Cropping' the image - the imaging area is physically smaller. The image remains the same size at the film plane and subject distance is the same – it is in no way magnified. This is great for macro photography as the net result is a much bigger image.

1/2 Types of Digital Cameras

CONSUMER CAMERAS – Entry Level

Consumer cameras distinguish themselves from professional Digital SLR cameras by having fixed zoom lenses. Within this group, there is commonly an additional distinction between entry-level cameras and "prosumer" cameras. Consumer cameras typically only offer very basic functions and controls and generally they are handy and compact in size. Great as a fun camera but if you are to go to the expense of housing one, the Prosumer cameras are better options.

PROSUMER CAMERAS

Prosumer cameras offer similar functions if not more features than DSLR professional cameras, but have limitations such as slower response time, smaller sensors and non-interchangeable lenses. Despite these limitations, prosumer cameras offer the advantage of being much easier to get started on… and much easier on the wallet too! Many glossy magazines have published images captured by prosumer cameras such as the Nikon Coolpix 8400, Sony F828 and Olympus 7070.

PROFESSIONAL Digital SLR CAMERAS

DSLR cameras overcome most of the limitations found in consumer models.

- Essentially all DSLR cameras offer the ability to use the same lenses as film SLR cameras. This allows for greater flexibility from super wide-angle 10.5mm to 105mm macro lenses. Sharper images result from the high quality lens optics.
- Response time is instantaneous – there is no shutter lag. If your goal is to capture the action ("dancing" clownfish, mating Mandarin fish, etc.), they are the way to go.
- There is greater latitude for controlling exposure inherent to the interchangeability of lenses.
- The size of the CCD or CMOS sensor is much larger, resulting in sharper pictures and much reduced field-of-view crop.

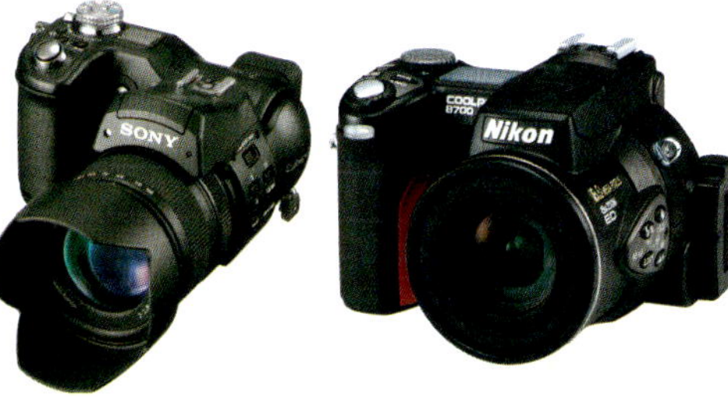

**PROSUMER series: Sony S828 &
Nikon Coopix 8000, 8 megapixel**

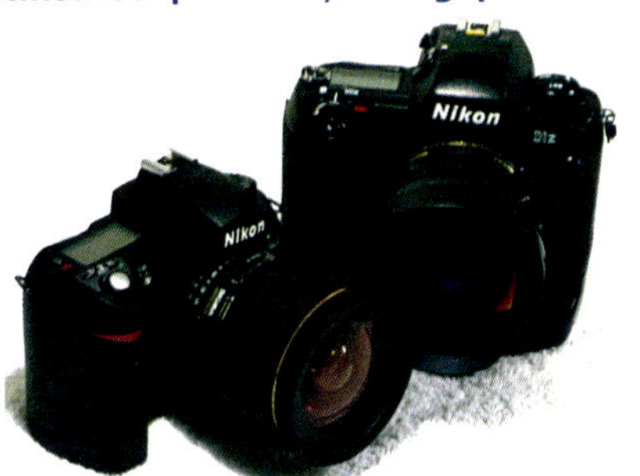

**Hi-end professional to serious
novice - Nikon D2X. D70s**

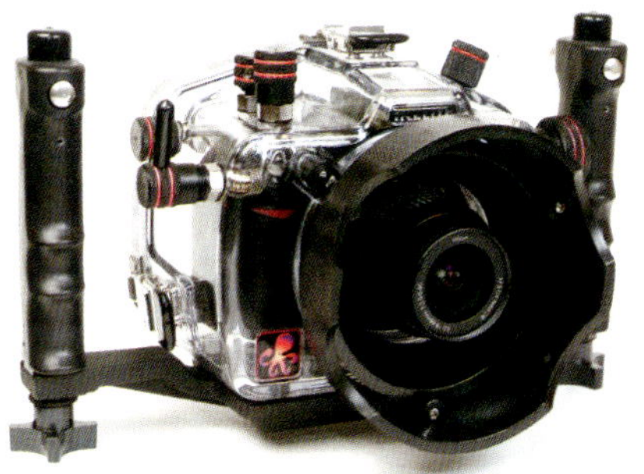

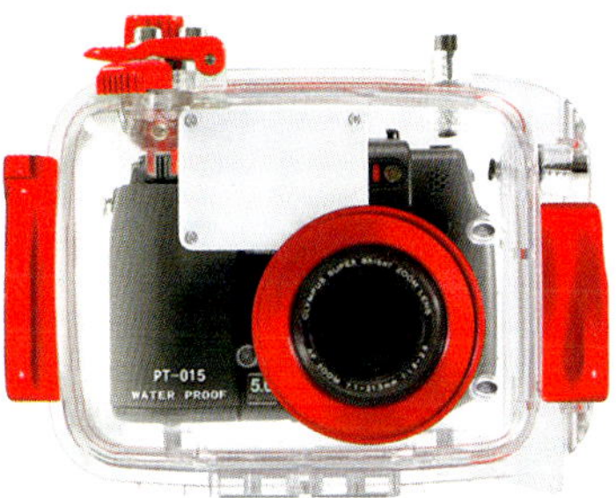

**Consumer series -
Olympus with housing**

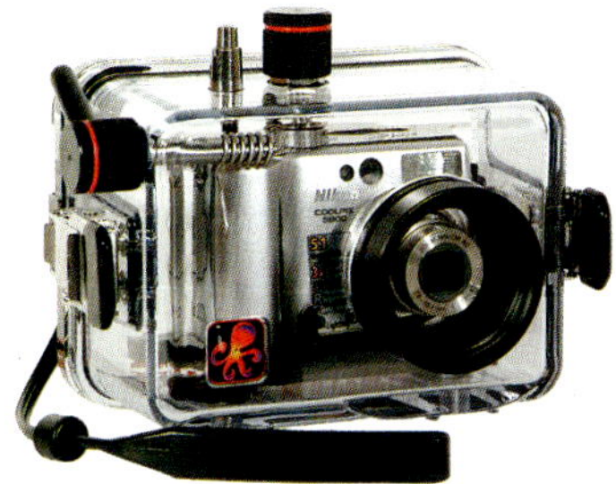

**Ikelite housings support a
wide range of digital cameras
- including the Nikon 7900**

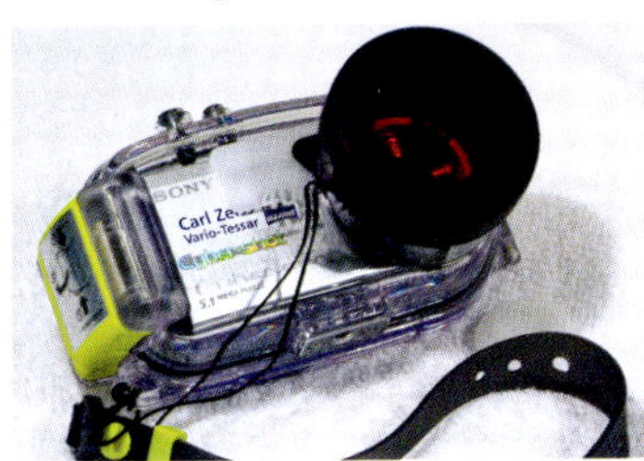

**CONSUMER series - Sony
Cybershot with housing**

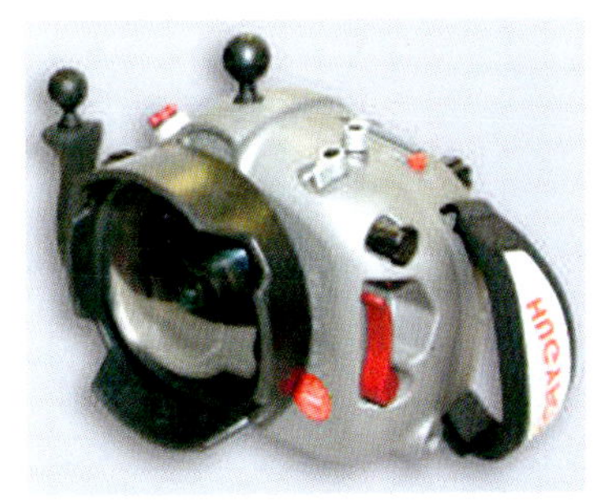

**Nikon and Canon SLR cameras are backed up by all the best housing
manufacturers - SEACAM, Ikelite, Hugyfot etc.**

Using an Underwater Housing

Before trying to shoot underwater it is imperative to get thoroughly familiar with all the controls on your camera on land first: you must learn to access all the necessary controls that you plan to use on your camera before you put the unit into the housing. Know them as well as you would know how to scratch your nose.

Next install the camera in the housing, close and check for seal integrity. (see 1/5). Now try to access all the functions you plan to use on your camera during a dive by playing with all the controls on the housing. If you dive with gloves, practise with them on. It is essential that you must be able to access the controls and perform the functions that you wish to use during a dive.

Housing Checklist:

1. On / Off switch – are you able to turn on and off?

2. Preview – set default to be 'ON' after each shot,
or access review by the push of a button.

3. On / Off macro – are you able to switch to macro mode?

4. Shooting Mode – are you able to change shooting mode A/S/M?

5. Flash mode – are you able to switch flash on and off?

6. Depending on shooting mode – try changing f-stops and shutter speed.

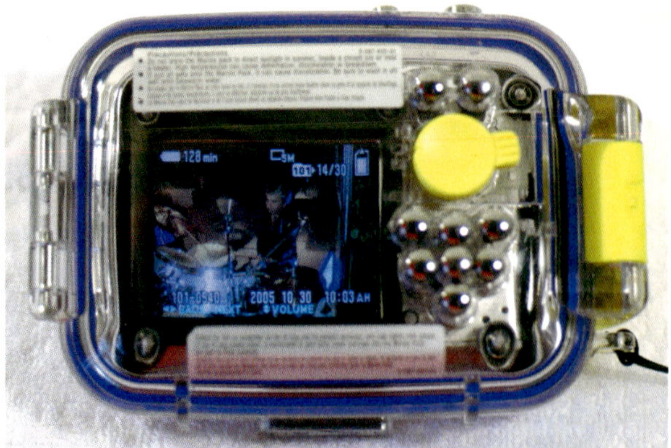

Test all controls are accessible before purchase; especially to change aperture, shutter speed, macro mode and review.

Critical Features for DSLR / Prosumer Housings:

1. Access buttons are spring loaded and work well at 30 metres and beyond.

2. Feature audio/ visual moisture alarm or easy view of seal integrity.

3. Option of 2nd bulk head.

4. Large viewfinder

5. Large controls

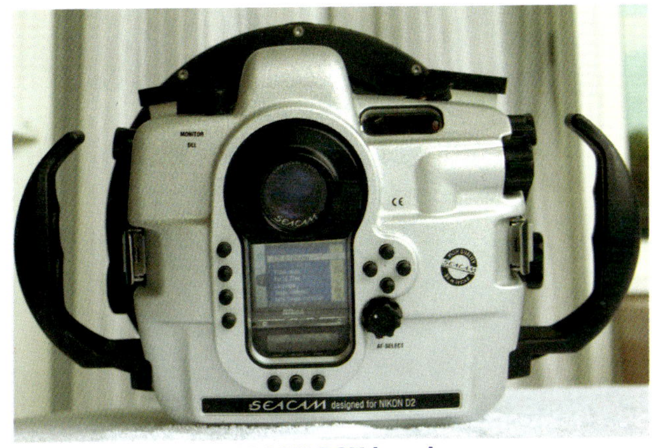

DSLR - SEACAM D2X housing

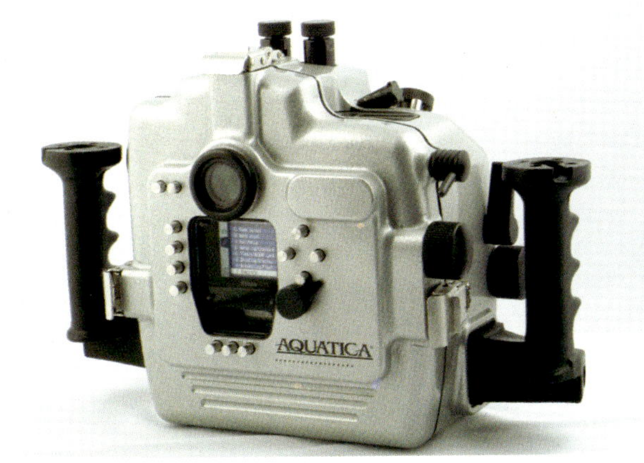

DSLR - AQUATICA D2X housing

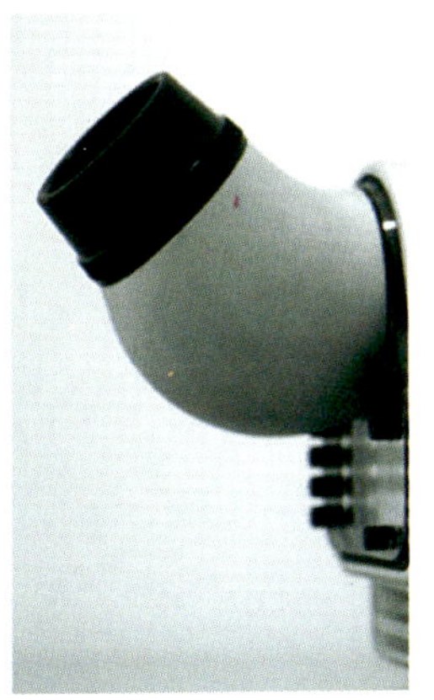

Seacam large S45 optical viewfinder

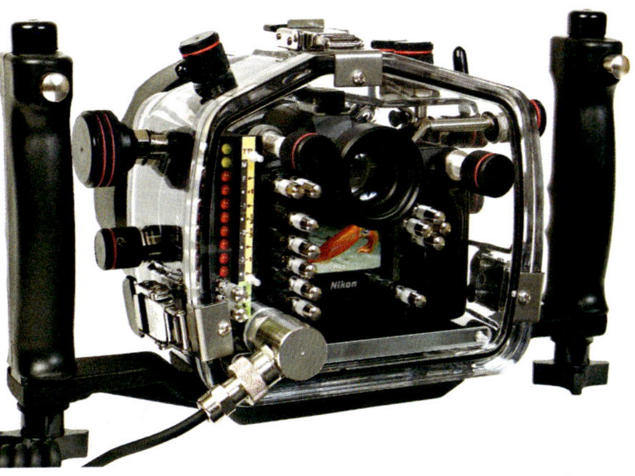

DSLR - Ikelite housing for NIKON D50

1/3 Understanding Exposure

Exposure is a term that refers to the total amount of light recorded by the camera's sensor for a given shot. This amount of light is influenced by three parameters: the aperture, shutter speed and sensitivity. If too much light is allowed to reach the sensor, the resulting shot will be overexposed (too bright). Conversely, if there isn't enough light recorded by the sensor, the shot will be too dark i.e. underexposed. In the first instance, closing down the aperture or using a faster shutter speed, or both, could resolve this problem. Similarly, for underexposed shots, using a slower shutter speed or larger aperture would help get a better exposure. Prior to taking a shot, the camera measures the amount of light in the frame and determines what should be the correct value for the aperture and shutter speed, based on the current sensitivity setting and metering mode. Metering actually refers to the process by which the camera measures the amount of light in one or several zones of the frame, and uses this information to set the parameters listed above.

DSLR and Prosumer cameras offer three common metering modes:

Matrix, 3D or Evaluative Metering:

This is the most complex of all metering modes. The frame is divided into a certain number of zones, for which the amount of light is measured individually. The camera then applies a proprietary algorithm to the collected information, and determines from there what the proper values of aperture and shutter speed should be. Because the algorithm used in this mode tries to achieve the best possible exposure for the entire picture, it gives the best results in most common situations, at least on land.

* In most situations, matrix metering does not work well underwater.

Centre-weighted Metering:

This mode is slightly different from the evaluative metering mode, in that although it measures light received in the entire frame, the greatest weight is assigned to an area in the centre of the frame when calculating exposure. This metering mode works well for portraits, when it is most important to properly expose a subject located in the centre of the frame, while retaining background detail.

* Centre-weighted is the most commonly used metering mode underwater.

Spot Metering:

When using spot metering, only light received from a small area in the centre of the frame is used to determine correct exposure. The light coming from the rest of the frame is ignored. This can be useful when shooting backlit or macro subjects. On high-end digital cameras, the location of the "spot" used for metering can be chosen as the focus point, giving the photographer more flexibility (e.g. shooting off-centre subjects).

** Spot metering works well when shooting extreme macro subjects.*

GETTING TO KNOW SHOOTING MODES

Most prosumer and professional cameras allow photographers to shoot in different modes. These modes dictate how much control the photographer has over the shooting parameters, versus how many of the latter are set by the camera.

The four most common modes offered by cameras are **P (or Auto), A, S, and M**. Some cameras (especially consumer cameras) may offer additional shooting modes, such as Night Scene, Portrait, Sports, etc. These modes are irrelevant to underwater photography.

Program Mode / Auto Mode:

We call this the PhD mode – PRESS HERE DUMMY. In these modes, the camera is set on "autopilot": it does a number of measurements (light levels, colours, distance to subject, etc) and automatically sets the aperture, shutter speed, focus and other parameters for the photographer. In some cameras, there is a Program (P) and an Auto mode. The only difference is that Auto is really fully automatic, while Program will still allows you make minor adjustments, such as setting the white balance, or forcing the flash on or off.

While Program / Auto modes work well on land. For underwater usage, they may work in some situations, but most of the time you will find that the shots do not turn out the way you wanted. In simplistic terms, program modes are programmed to handle lighting conditions on land, not underwater.

Aperture Priority or A Mode:

A Mode means that the camera lets you set the aperture manually, but determines what it thinks is the correct shutter speed automatically. This can be useful in a certain number of situations. For example, if you set a very large aperture (small number, e.g. f/2 or f/2.8), the depth of field will be greatly reduced. This in turn will make your subject stand out clearly against a blurred background. Typically, film photographers use this mode when shooting macro subjects – it works well for digital too. Macro lenses and the Macro mode in prosumer cameras reduce the DOF (depth-of-field), making it necessary to adopt a small aperture (large number, e.g. f/16 or f/22) to get as much of the subject in focus. This is probably the mode of choice for most conditions. With the ability to control both the amount of light entering the camera and the DOF, you can cover almost any situation with the aperture-priority mode.

NOTE: Whilst it is not a problem for DSLR camera users, there is one major limitation for users of Consumer/Prosumer cameras using Aperture Priority mode. Most cameras in the these ranges only offer aperture settings of f/2.8 to f/8 – this gives the photographer only 4 to 5 settings to choose from. For such cameras, Shutter priority mode offers better exposure control.

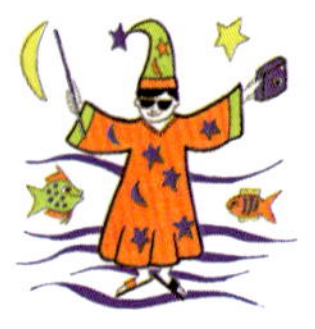

How to set up to shoot with A mode:

1. Check that A mode is clearly indicated on the LCD screen or viewfinder.

2. Set ISO (film speed equivalent) to 100 or the lowest possible.

3. For wide-angle with DSLR camera select f/11 and prosumer camera select f/8 as a starting point. For macro with DSLR camera select f/22 and prosumer camera select f/11 (if available) as a starting point.

4. If using external strobe, start with 1/2 power if available.

5. Position yourself about 1 metre in front of desired subject.

6. Shoot and review. Dial up (bigger number) the aperture if image is too bright or dial down (smaller number) if image is too dark. Or bracket with strobe power. Use whichever is faster to change.

Better Understanding of Aperture

Imagine the f-stop / aperture to be a gate in a paddock. The smaller the gate / large number f-stop (e.g. f/8, f/11, f/22) the less cows (light) will be able to rush through when the gate is open and shut momentarily. Conversely, the bigger the gate / small number f-stop (e.g. f/4, f/2) the more cows (light) will be able to rush through when the gate is open and shut momentarily.

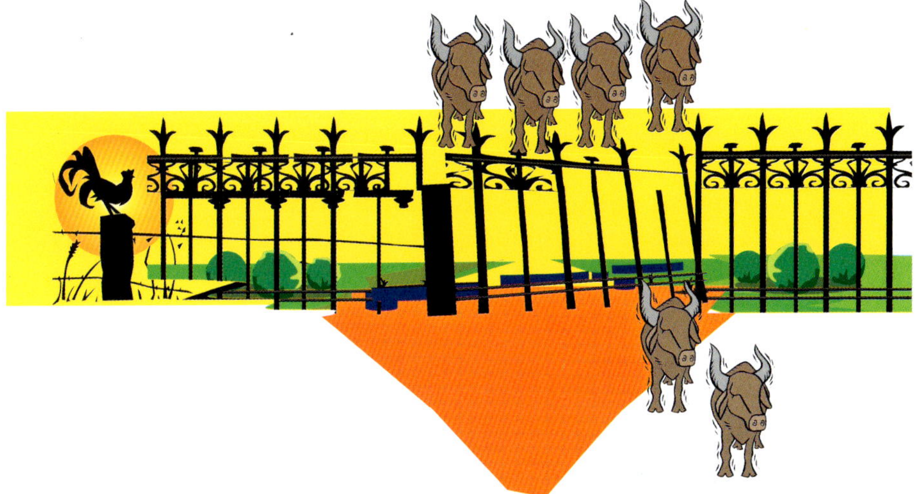

Large number f-stop (eg f11, f16) =
small gate open = less cows (LIGHT) rush in.

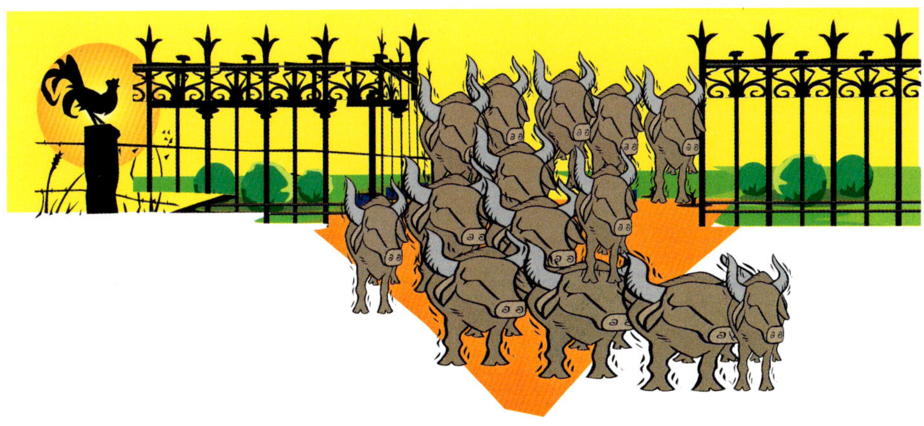

Small number f-stop (eg f2.8. f4,) =
big gate open = more cows (LIGHT) rush in.

Shutter Priority - S Mode:

Essentially in S mode, you set the shutter speed, and let the camera figure out the required aperture. This can be used to achieve a number of effects. For example, if you want to shoot a fast-moving marine creature, you can set the shutter-speed to a faster value (e.g. 1/125s or 1/250s). This will freeze the action, and give you a sharp image. For prosumer camera users, the S mode offers a better selection for exposure setting. While the A mode is generally restricted between f/2 to f/8, in most of the latest prosumer camera shutter speed setting allows for 1/30s to 1/3200s in 1/3 stop increments! This range is very useful, especially when shooting in extreme lighting conditions – in dark water or early morning. Generally speaking, the S mode works better with an external strobe for which the power intensity can also be adjusted.

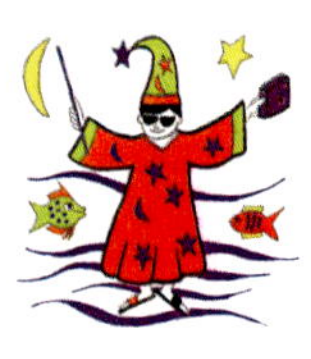

How to set up to shoot with S mode:

1. Check that S mode is clearly indicated on the LCD screen or viewfinder.

2. Set ISO (film speed equivalent) to 100 or the lowest possible.

3. For DSLR cameras select 1/60s and prosumer cameras select 1/125s as a starting point.

4. If you are shooting with an external strobe, start with 1/2 power if available.

5. Bracket your shots by adjusting the speed setting or strobe setting, whichever is faster to manage.

6. Position yourself about 1 metre in front of desired subject.

7. Shoot and review in LCD. Dial up for faster speed if image is too bright or dial down for slower shutter speed if exposure is too dark. Remember the faster the speed, the darker the water. For lighter blue background, use slower speed and compensate by powering down the strobe.

NOTE: With some cameras, strobes may only sync with a shutter speed of up to 1/250s. If the shutter speed is too fast, you will end up with an underexposed image or only half of the image exposed.

Better Understanding of shutter speed

Imagine shutter speed to be the speed the paddock gate opens and closes. The faster the shutter speed (e.g. 1/250s, 1/500s), the faster the gate opens and closes, thus the less cows (light) will be able to rush into the paddock. Conversely, the slower the gate opens and closes, the slower the shutter speed (e.g. 1/30s), the more cows (light) will be able to rush through into the paddock.

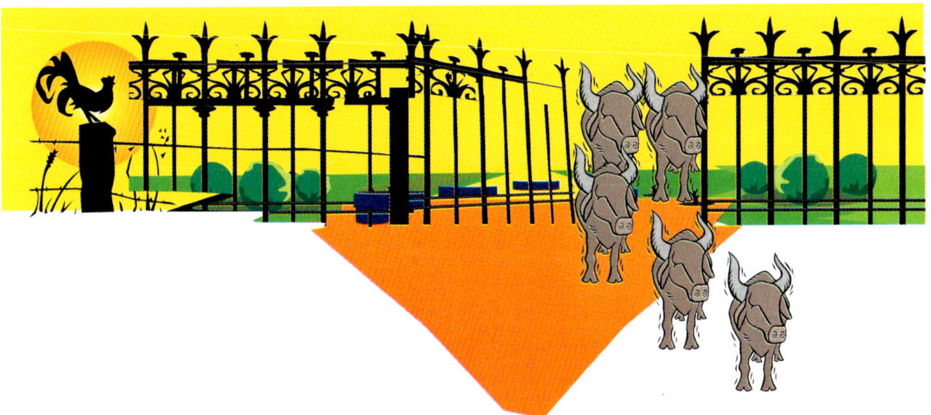

Fast shutter speed (eg 1/250 sec, 1/500 sec,) = gate opens & closes quickly = less cows (LIGHT) rush in.

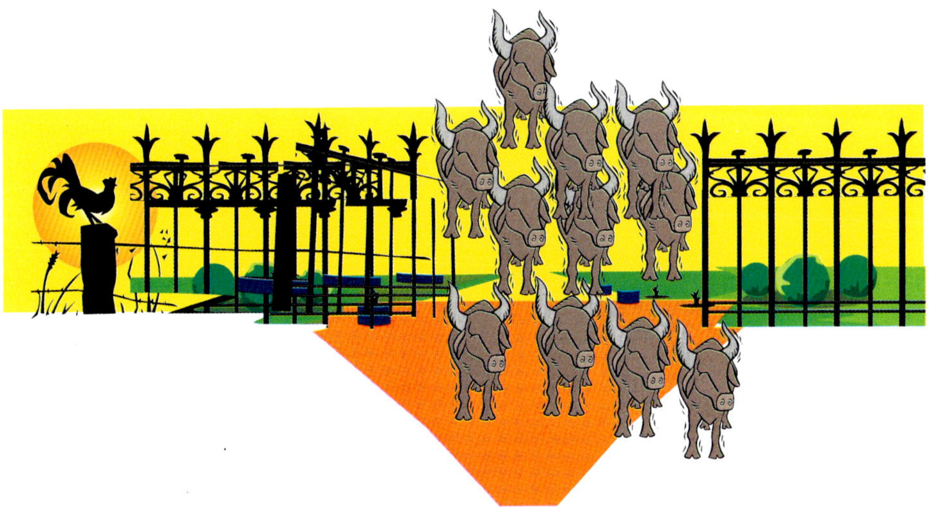

Slow shutter speed (eg 1/15 sec, 1/30 sec,) = gate opens & closes slowly = more cows (LIGHT) rush in.

Manual - M Mode:

Manual mode may be the most complex but it is here that you assume full control of the result of your pictures. You can adjust the aperture and the shutter speed, as well as all the other parameters (focus, white balance, exposure value, etc.) This mode is the most versatile, as you can use it to achieve the same result as with any other mode.

Sometimes, the camera's internal light meter may not work correctly, or may be fooled by the composition in some situations (e.g. shooting from inside a wreck or cave towards the outside). In this case, shooting in aperture-priority mode will give an over-exposed subject, while shooting in shutter-priority mode may require apertures larger than what the camera is capable of. In this case, shooting in manual mode is the only option.

One point to note with some 'intelligent' cameras is when you set the aperture or the shutter speed in manual mode, the camera will tell you what it thinks the other parameter should be. This is done using colour codes or using a numbered scale. (Refer to camera manual). You can use this first 'guess' made by the camera and bracket your exposure one stop over and one stop under the recommendation. At the time of writing, few camera, strobe and housing combinations are capable of TTL exposure (see Module 2). As such most DSLR and consumer/prosumer camera users are balancing the final exposure by use of shutter speed and or aperture setting with the intensity of the external strobe. In this context, the use of manual mode to control both aperture and shutter speed gives the best control of the end result.

How to set up to shoot with M mode:

1. Check that M mode is clearly indicated on the LCD screen or viewfinder. Set ISO (film speed equivalent) to 100 or the lowest possible.

2. For DSLR select shutter speed to 1/60s and aperture to f/8 and prosumer cameras select shutter speed to 1/60s and aperture to f/5.6 as a starting point.

3. If using external strobe, start with 1/2 power if available.

4. Position yourself about 1 metre in front of desired subject.

5. Shoot and review. Bracket your shots by adjusting the speed setting, aperture or strobe setting whichever is easier to manage.

Variations – assuming ISO is set at 100, and a picture is correctly exposed with aperture f/5.6 and shutter speed of 1/60s, by manipulating exposure settings we will still be able to achieve a correctly exposed image but with a different aesthetic quality.

• For a pictures with a lighter blue background, shallow DOF expose by using f/4 aperture and shutter speed of 1/125s.

• For a more contrasting picture with greater DOF expose with f/8 aperture and a shutter speed of 1/30s.

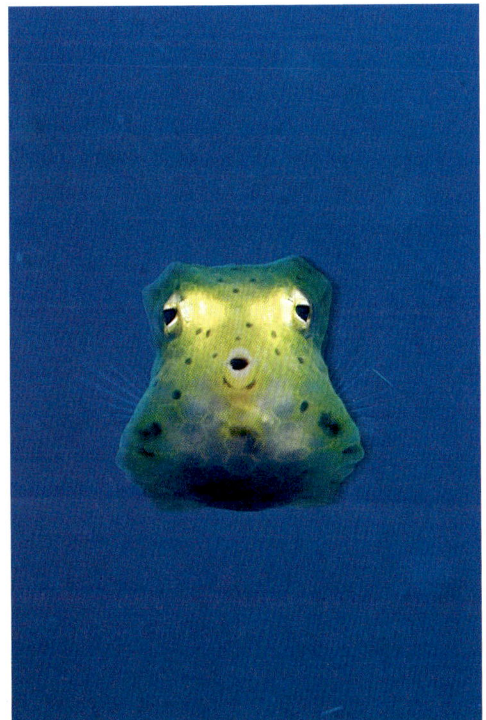

**f5.6, 1/125s Strobe 1/2 power
blue background - less sharp**

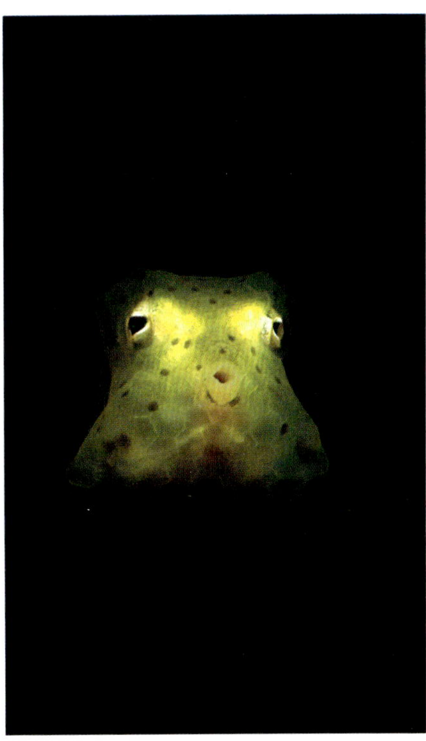

**f11, 1/60s Strobe full power
black background - sharper**

Better Understanding of M mode

In manual mode, you are really controlling how fast or slow the gate is open and shut and as well as the size of gate to determine how many cows (amount of light) to enter in each instance. In a way, you are controlling how your cows (light) are positioned in the paddock too!

Understanding and Setting WHITE BALANCE

Digital camera sensors are designed to detect light. They can tell what is bright and what is dark, but they cannot distinguish between colours. To establish colours in the picture, the sensor is fitted with an array of tiny coloured filters, called (surprise!) Colour Filter Arrays (CFA). These come in different variations: GRGB (Green, Red, Green, Blue) or CMYK (Cyan, Magenta, Yellow, Black), which eliminate all colours but that of the filter itself.

To establish what white is, the camera uses the white balance system. Depending on the white balance setting selected on the camera, the built-in software adds a certain hue to the picture to compensate for different lighting conditions. For example, if you look at a white wall that is lit by an incandescent light (normal light bulb), it will appear yellow. But if you set the 'Incandescent' white balance on your camera and take a shot of that wall, it will appear white. What the camera has effectively done is to put a pale bluish tint to the entire picture to compensate for the yellow light, resulting in a white wall on the photo.

Most digital cameras come with some preset white balances: sunny, cloudy, incandescent, tungsten, etc. The default setting, however, is 'Automatic' white balance. In this mode, the camera analyses the picture and determines what it thinks is the best white balance setting for this particular shot. This works well when using a strobe or other external light source to light up the subject. However, when taking shots with ambient light, the automatic white balance may not work properly. Underwater, past a certain depth, the light is predominantly blue. This tends to fool the automatic white balance of the camera, resulting either in blue shots, or in bright white patches on the picture. One way to get around this problem is to set a 'Custom' white balance.

For the underwater photographer, this can be done by taking along a white slate, and using it to calibrate the white balance underwater. As the lighting conditions varies with the depth and time of the day, you would need to re-measure the white balance regularly. However in practice, setting a white balance at an average depth once should be sufficient, as further adjustments to the colour and exposure can be done in post-processing (see Module 4).

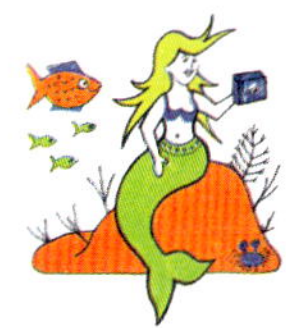

HINTS

1. Instead of taking a slate down and doing a custom white balance underwater, a quick fix can be to use a white piece of paper, and to set your white balance at night under a neon light (the bluish white type). This results in a reddish tint that should work well for most conditions underwater.

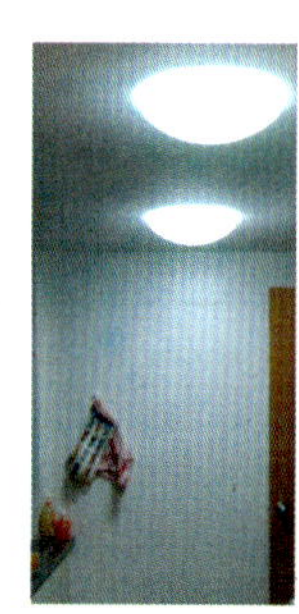

2. Use Auto White Balance - fix up in editing software (see module 4).

UNDERSTANDING and Setting FLASH MODES

Prosumer Cameras

All prosumer digital cameras come with a built-in flash. This flash is normally meant for land photography, and is not very powerful. As light is absorbed quickly with depth, these built-in flashes have a very limited range (typically effective to less than 1 metre). To make things worse they are fixed to the camera, very close to the lens. This will frequently result in backscatter (see Module 2 for more on this topic). To help prevent this, underwater housing manufacturers now fit housings with diffusers that help tone down the light from the flash, thereby reducing backscatter, but also further decreasing light intensity. This means that underwater, the built-in flash is only useful for close-up shots (say, less than 0.5m).

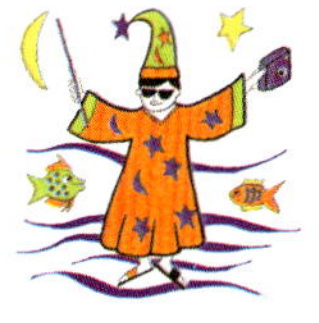

How to Set Flash Mode

Consumer / Prosumer USER – without external flash
1. Close up shot – set FLASH to always ON.

2. Wider Angle shot of more than 1 metre distance – turn flash off.

Consumer / Prosumer USER with external flash
If you are using an optical slave system, set flash to always on.

DSLR USER
DSLR systems require the use of an external strobe. The camera will automatically detect the strobe once it is powered on.

Setting RESOLUTION and IMAGE QUALITY

A common misconception is that a camera offering a higher resolution will always give better results than a camera with a lower resolution. This is not necessarily the case. Aside from the photographer's skill, the quality of a shot depends mostly on the quality of the optics, the quality of the sensor, and the image-processing chip used by the camera. The resolution itself is only a count of how many dots of light are recorded by the sensor. Besides the quality of the optics, the format that the picture is recorded in has a direct bearing on the quality of the final picture. This is normally referred to as the "Picture Format", "Image Size" and "Quality" settings on a digital camera.

"Picture Format" refers to the type of file that is written on the camera's storage device. There are typically 3 different types of file format: RAW, TIFF and JPEG.

RAW format saves the information recorded by the sensor exactly as it is – details are sharper and edges are smoother than other formats. This type of file requires processing with proprietary software.

TIFF format represents an actual image, including colour and exposure compensation, as imposed by the camera.

JPEG format is the same as the TIFF format, except that it compresses the information to save space on storage cards. JPEG images average the picture information, typically based on an 8 pixel by 8 pixel grid, resulting in coarser details, and more or less jagged edges. The first two formats result in the best quality, but at the expense of very large files, and thus less possible pictures for a given storage card size, as well as slower recording time, especially on consumer cameras. A JPEG image typically takes much less space than a RAW or TIFF file, but at the expense of quality.

"Image Size" parameter refers to how many of the image-recording dots in the sensor are used to create the picture. This normally applies only to the JPEG image format. At the highest setting, most of the image sensor is used to form the image. At lower settings, the image will comprise of less dots or pixels, the rest of the sensor information being discarded. This will have an influence on how much editing you can do on your picture, and how large a print you can obtain (refer to Module 4 for more on this topic).

"Quality" setting also normally only applies to JPEG images. This parameter dictates how much compression is applied to the picture, and therefore how detailed or coarse the final picture is. As such an image shot in "Normal" quality will be coarser, but smaller in size, than a picture in "SHQ" or "High Quality" format.

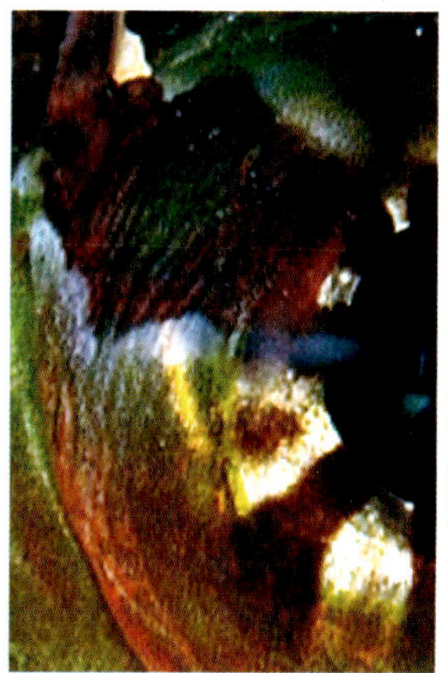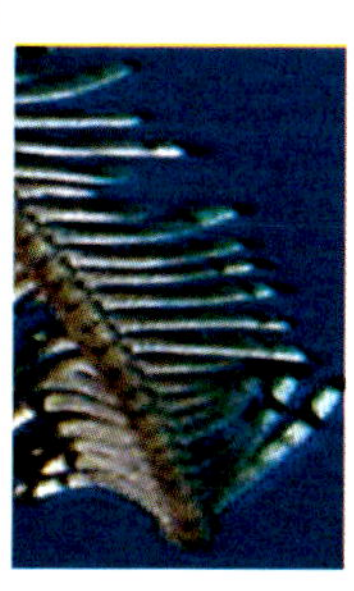

Jpeg Best Quality: FINE @300%

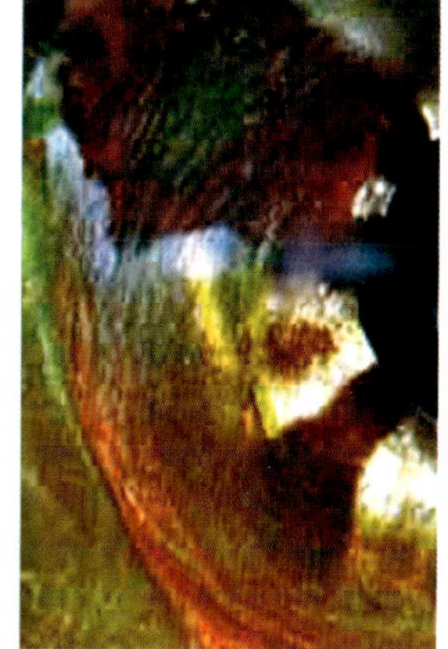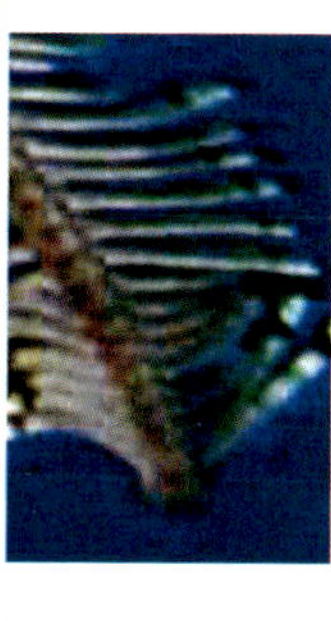

Jpeg Lowest Quality: Standard @300%

If you want the best quality for your pictures, set your camera to shoot in RAW format. Given that the cost of media keeps dropping, the number of pictures that can be taken in a single dive should not be an issue, as you can always get higher capacity storage media. This setting will give the best results if you intend to print your pictures. However, if you mostly review your pictures on your computer, or mostly create slideshows, then shooting in highest quality JPEG is sufficient. Shooting pictures in RAW format allows you to efficiently process pictures adjusting exposure, white balance, hue, saturation and sharpening with little or no degradation. (see Module 4)

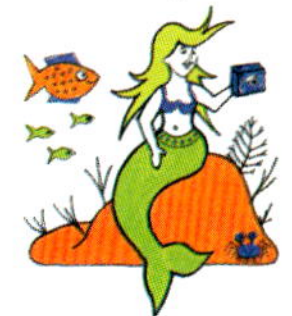

HINTS

1. DSLR users – shoot RAW mode. Prosumer users – shoot in a jpeg mode with the least compression.

2. DSLR users – a 1GB card. Prosumer users - get a 256MB or a 512MB card.

3. Download the card after each dive and reformat it for the next dive. The inevitable will happen, so beat the odds.

4. Make sure you have a couple of storage cards as backup.

1/4 The Digital Photographer – Back Up

Extra Batteries: Digital cameras (and strobes) are power hungry. The greatest frustration is to run out of batteries during a dive. The best option is to use rechargeable Ni-MH or Li-Ion batteries with a high mAh rating. Ni-MH batteries are the most common type of rechargeable batteries. They typically offer high capacities, but have long recharge times (normally 6 to 12 hours). Camera-specific batteries (proprietary batteries) are typically Li-Ion batteries. They are usually characterised by lower capacities than Ni-MH batteries, but much faster recharging times (between 1 and 2 hours). Regardless of the type of batteries accepted by your camera, it is a good idea to bring 1 or 2 spare batteries if you go on extended dive trips, as it may not be possible to recharge batteries during the day, between dives.

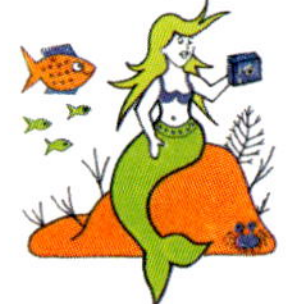

HINTS

1. Always bring one to two back-up batteries.

2. Mark each battery with your name and the date of first use.

3. Always use a freshly charged battery for the first dive of the day.

4. When conducting battery check before a dive, turn on the camera, leave it on for 5 minutes even if the battery gauge is showing a fully charged battery. This allows the capacitor to stabilise to give a more reliable indication.

5. Between dive trips, store batteries in the fridge. This helps extend the working life of rechargeable batteries.

Storage Media Cards: The next most frustrating thing after running out of batteries is running out of storage space. The storage media cards bundled with the camera are often not sufficient to allow you to take underwater shots through an entire dive. Since it is not possible to swap storage cards during a dive, it is useful to buy one or two large capacity storage cards. There are currently more than 8 different types of storage cards (CompactFlash / MicroDrive, SmartMedia, MemoryStick, xD Picture Card, etc.). The idea is buy the biggest capacity - Memory Stick now available in 1-2 gig and CF compact and Micro Drive 2-5 gigs.

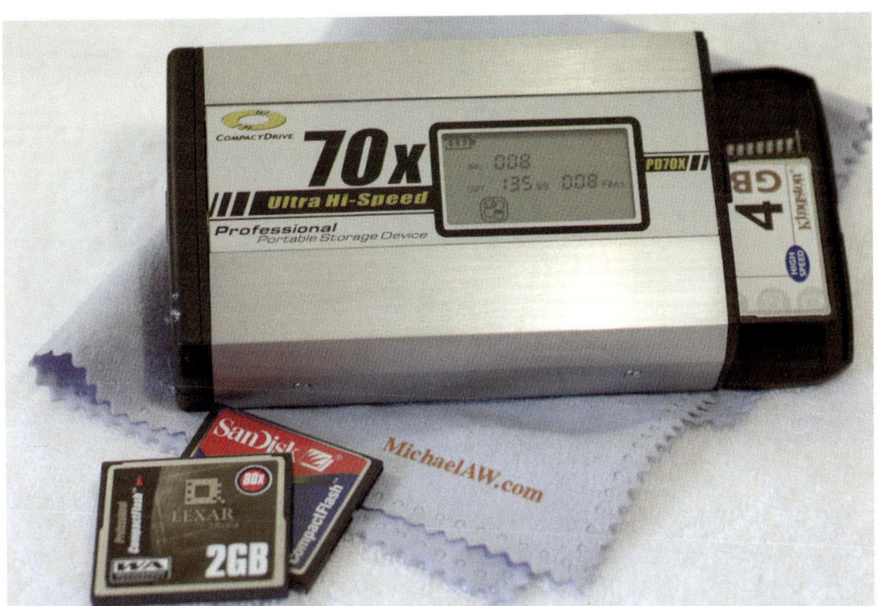

Portable Storage Devices: These devices allow digital photographers to transfer the contents of their storage media cards onto a portable large capacity hard drive, without the need for a personal computer. This can be especially useful for going on extended trips when you are not carrying your notebook computer around, or when you don't have the opportunity to download pictures during the day and have insufficient space on your storage card for an entire day of shooting. Features to look out for in these devices include the ability to read different types of cards, simple operation, and a USB 2.0 or FireWire interface. You will find the latter can save you several hours in downloading time when you come back from a long dive trip. Some of these devices come with an LCD screen that allows you to review stored pictures. This may sound like a worthy option at first, but this review is typically extremely slow (much slower than in the camera), and normally does not support RAW or TIFF files. For these reasons, the additional LCD screen may not be worth the extra cost.

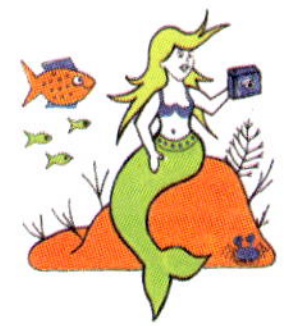

HINTS

1. If you are investing in a portable storage device, go for one with at least 40GB capacity, with USB 2.0 or FireWire interface.

2. Hard drives do fail – back up all your files on CD or DVD upon return from each trip.

Storage Media Card Reader: allows direct transfer of files from the storage media card to the computer. This helps preserve camera battery life, and is much faster than downloading from the camera. Make sure it is a USB 2.0 or FireWire interface, and that it reads most common types storage cards.

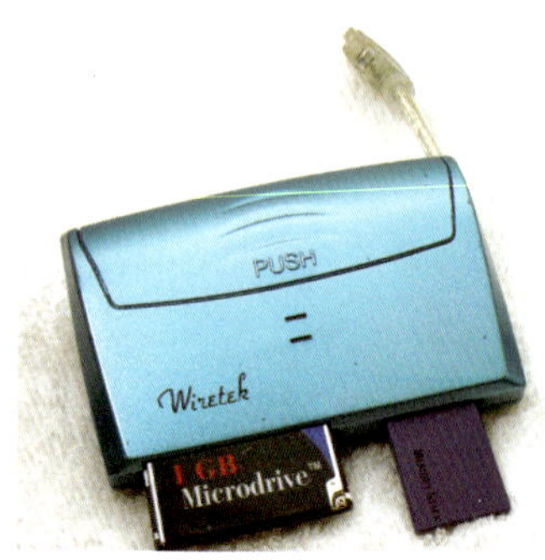

Wrist Strap: this is an absolute essential. Make sure you use it and it is strong. There may be time when you may need both hands to perform other important tasks. It is a good idea to have a quick release D ring to secure your camera on your BCD. The ideal position for attaching a wrist strap is on the same side as the shutter release.

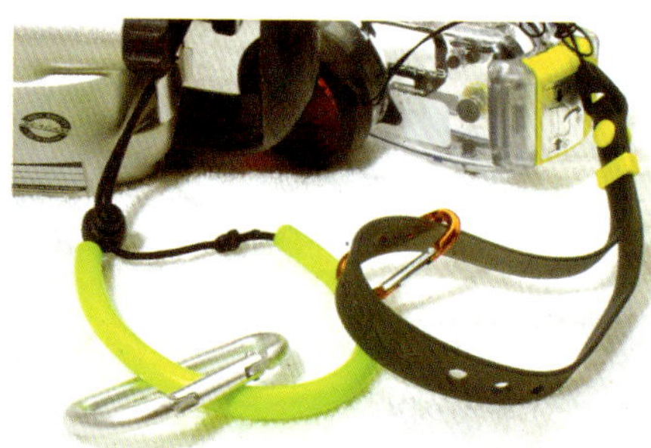

Carry Case: Lugging all this expensive and fragile equipment around can prove to be a logistical nightmare. The safest solution is to use a padded carry case (Lowe Pro AW Tracker / Pelican recommended). You should get a case that has plenty of room for future expansion, is crush-proof and waterproof.

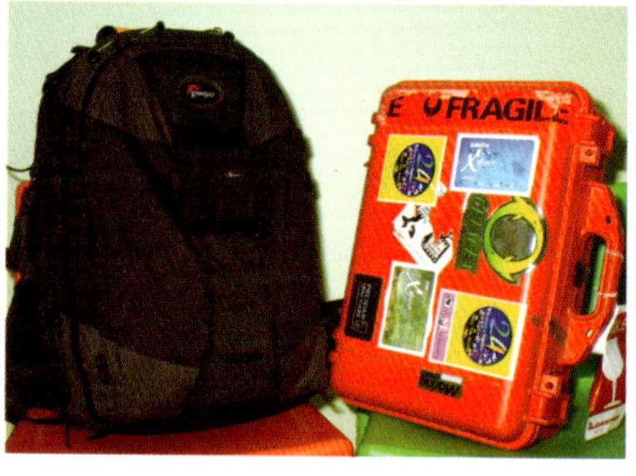

Leak Detector Alarm: If your housing offers a leak alarm as an option, insist on having it. This small investment may just save your camera and lens. High end DSLR housings such as SEACAM's leak alarm system are both audio and visual. This is the most desirable warning system in housing technology.

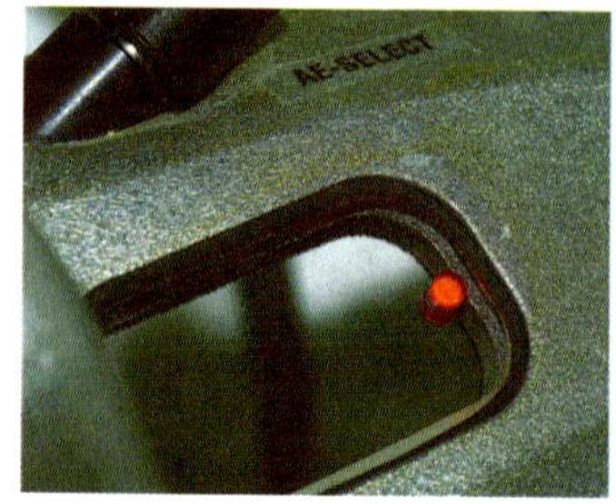

Fogging Problems

Consumer digital cameras heat up very quickly often resulting in condensation inside small polycarbonate housings. Some housing manufacturers include a small bottle of "anti-fog" solution with the housing. This is meant to be applied to the inside of the housing lens prior to the dive. Another alternative is to place small packs of desiccant inside the housing prior to the dive, so as to absorb moisture. This works best when the sachets are placed in the housing well ahead of time.

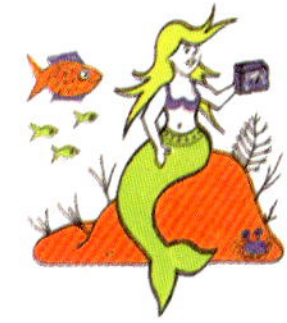

HINTS

1. Apply defogging agent sparingly – if it works, a light coat will suffice.

2. Do not assemble camera in air-conditioned room.

3. Do not leave camera housing in direct sunlight

4. Immersing the housed camera with the lens facing up in the rinse tank before a dive helps in preventing condensation on the lens.

5. If budget avails, switch to a larger housing e.g. Ikelite or Aquatica.

O-rings Seal Integrity: in order to be watertight, all underwater housings are fitted with o-rings. They are the primary defence against flood. It is essential to take good care of o-rings. There are two main types of o-rings: removable and non-removable ones. Removable o-rings are typically used as perimeter seals for the housing "door", and for ports. Non-removable o-rings are normally used to seal button shafts, sliders and other moving parts.

In order to make operation smooth and avoid pinching removable o-rings, some housing manufacturers recommend greasing them with silicone grease. If this is the recommended procedure for your housing, avoid being over-generous with this silicone grease. **A very light coat will do the job – remember grease does not prevent flooding – a clean o-ring does.** While in theory it is beneficial to the operation of the housing, it can also contribute to attracting dirt or sand, often resulting in floods. Thus it is ESSENTIAL to visually inspect o-rings thoroughly each time you open the back of the housing. In most cases, it is not necessary to grease o-rings before every dive. Once at the beginning of a diving day or a diving weekend should be sufficient.

IMPORTANT NOTES

1. When using a brand new housing, or even a secondhand one, take the housing for a dive – without the camera. This is your best prevention against a nasty surprise!

2. If you have your housing in storage for more than 6 months, it is also a good idea to do your first dive without the camera. You never know, especially in the tropics: o-rings do perish or your pet mouse may have mistaken it for cheese!

3. When not used over an extended period, it is a good habit to remove the main o-ring from the housing during storage.

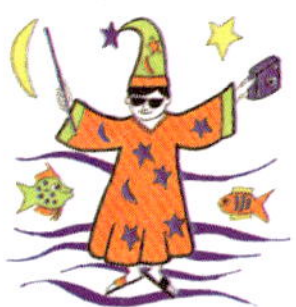

How to conduct Pre-dive checks

1. Inspect o-rings. Remove user serviceable o-rings from the housing and visually inspect for nicks, dents, scratches, dirt, sand, hair and fluff.

2. Gently wipe them clean with a white worn out towel.

3. Lightly grease the o-ring with the manufacturers recommended silicon grease.

4. Re-install them into their respective tracks or grooves. Visually check that they are sited properly and free of foreign particles.

5. Install the camera, test all the controls and fire once or twice to check that all settings are as intended.

6. Before the dive, submerge the entire unit in a rinse tank – check for bubbles. Remember to play with the controls and fire again to check that the unit is ready to work underwater.

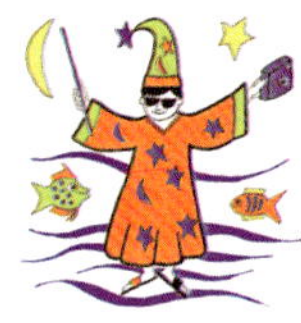

How to conduct Post-dive checks

1. Rinse the camera unit in the rinse tank – do not just leave the unit in the tank. Dip and Dunk the unit a few times.

2. Play with the controls to ensure the shafts are clean of sea water.

3. Store in a dry place – remove storage media and download immediately.

Flooded housing

If you see a small stream of bubbles coming from your housing during a dive, the seal integrity has failed.

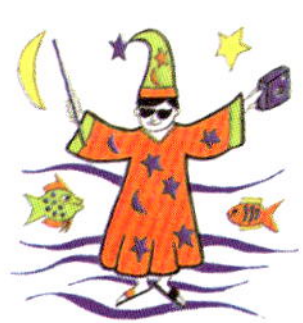

How to React during a FLOOD

1. Orientate your housing port to face down.

2. Signal your buddy to ascend with you and begin a controlled emergency ascent. You should

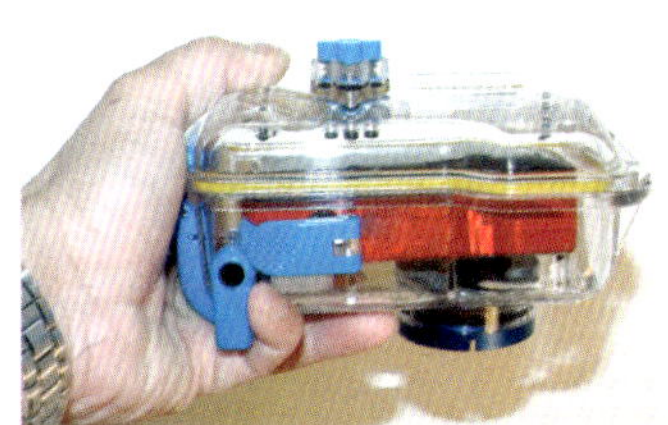

be proficient with this procedure – otherwise refer to your scuba manual and seek a refresher from your scuba instructor.

3. You may opt for a normal ascent or continue the dive since digital cameras are very sensitive to water. In most cases replacement is the only option. The decision is entirely yours – make an educated choice.

4. Once at the surface, try to raise the housing above water maintaining the port/lens down position until help arrives. When passing the camera up to the boat, insist that the port down position is maintained.

5. Dry yourself and immediately open the back of the housing and remove the camera. Remove the battery and media storage card. For DSLR cameras, remove the lens from the body.

6. If you notice that the camera body especially the battery and storage card compartment are drenched with sea water, then you may have to make a very quick decision. Immerse the entire body in a bucket of fresh water and give it a quick swish, dip and dunk.

7. If there are just few droplets of water, you may choose to use a clean cloth, wet it with clean fresh water and dry the affected area.

8. You may opt to use a small hair dryer and gently blow dry the camera. Make sure the camera is wiped dry and the dryer setting is on low and positioned at least 10 inches away from the camera body when blowing.

9. Once you are satisfied that there is no water residue in the camera, replace the battery and power on. If there's no sign of life, pack the unit and send for professional assessment.

10. Rinse the housing interior with fresh water – place the housing in a bath tub and check for bubbles. Identify problematic area, replace the o-ring and repeat the test in the bath tub. Take the housing for a dive without the camera.

11. If there's no leak, take the housing for a dive. Only dive with a camera installed when you are 100% satisfied that the seal integrity has been restored. ***You should send the housing for a pressure test after a major flood.***

Flooded sync cord bulkhead

One of the most common problems that happen with housed camera systems is a flooded sync cord bulkhead. Although proper pre-dive and post-dive care and regular maintenance should prevent such occurrence, by design fault, some bulkheads are more prone to leakage. If your strobe starts behaving erratically underwater, firing intermittently, you may have a flooded sync cord bulkhead.

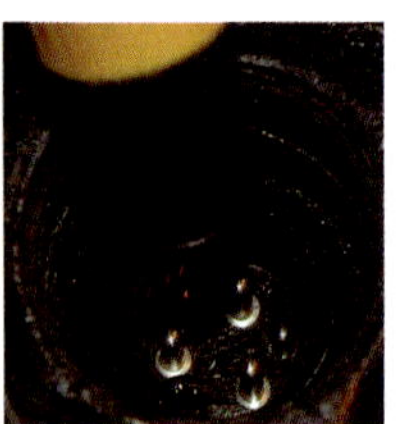

Blow dry the bulkhead with blower.

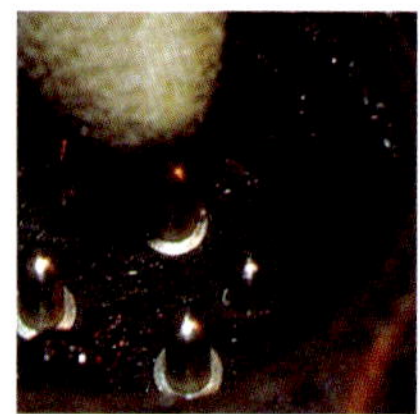

Dry off with make-up applicator.

How to treat a flooded sync cord

1. As soon as possible immerse housing in fresh water, then dry and disconnect sync cord.

2. Check for moisture inside the bulkhead. If a leak is confirmed, rinse the bulkhead with a few drops of fresh water to prevent salt build-up and corrosion of the connector pins.

3. Finally, dry the bulkhead thoroughly using a pneumatic blower, or dry off with a mini hair dryer and make-up applicator.

4. Repeat the same for the connector end of the sync chord. With this method you should be able to salvage your flooded connector.

5. Find out the reason for the leak, such as a nick on the o-ring. Change if required.

HINT – beat the odds – **if the option is available, fit a second bulkhead to your housing.**

Post-dive trip care

Following a dive trip several things can happen to your system: salt, sand and silt can lodge themselves in hinges or button assemblies, water can dry on external lenses, damaging any surface coatings in the process, electrolytic reactions can continue taking place between the different metallic components of your system, etc.

1. In order to stop these from happening and prevent any long-term damage to your system, you should soak the whole system in lukewarm fresh water for 15 minutes after completing a multi day dive trip.

2. Once you have removed your system from the tub, make sure you dry all external lenses you may use with a clean and lint-free cloth.

3. Disassemble any components which are made of dissimilar metals (e.g. steel tray and aluminium housing), to stop electrolytic reactions from happening. If you do not follow this recommendation, you may find that after a while, these components cannot be separated.

4. If you are putting away the housing for storage, remove the main o-ring – this will ensure that it retains its elasticity. Similarly, before flying, you should also remove the o-ring to prevent pressure build up inside the housing, resulting in the o-ring being squashed.

5. Better still: use a set of o-rings for travel and storage and a set for diving.

6. If you are living in a humid tropical country, store the camera and lenses in a dedicated dry cabinet. This will minimise risks of the electronics deteriorating, and fungus forming inside the lenses.

Note: Silica gel packs keep absorbing moisture as long as they are exposed to it. In order to extend their life span and efficiency, you should keep them all in a small sealed Ziploc bag between dives or dive trips. Make sure to flatten the Ziploc bag to remove as much air as possible before sealing them. This will further extend the life span of the silica gel. It can also be recharged by drying in a warm oven or microwave.

Field Maintenance Essentials

The first component for a field maintenance kit is a small white body towel. The best type is the camping towel (made of viscose rayon), since they are small and light, but can absorb a lot of water and dry really fast. This towel is used to lay down your system before field maintenance.

These are suggested items that you will use in the field at one time or another. You should have them all in your tool box:

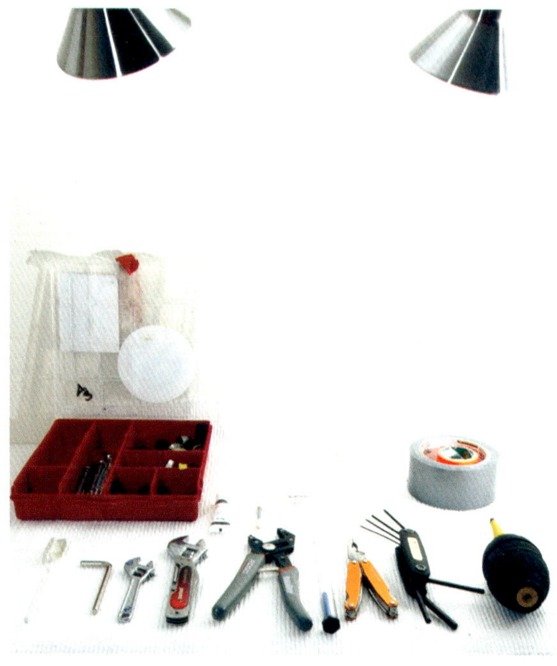

Silicone grease: it may be required to maintain the integrity of o-rings. Always follow the manufacturer's recommendations when selecting which type of silicone grease to use.

Anti-fog solution: it is applied to the inside of the housing lens to prevent condensation. This is especially useful when diving in cold water.

Make-up sponge applicator: these are a much better option than cotton buds – they are fluff free and re-usable.

White face towel: to wipe the housing and do general cleaning; the white towels from Singapore Airlines are particularly suitable for this task!

Lint-free cloth or lens paper: these are used to clean the housing lens without leaving any particles or stains.

Additional items:

- Multi tool Swiss Army knife (make sure you pack it in your main luggage not your carry-on!)
- Allen key set
- C-wrench or adjustable spanner
- Spare o-rings – housing, strobes, sync cord
- Battery tester
- Small hair dryer
- Precision screwdriver set

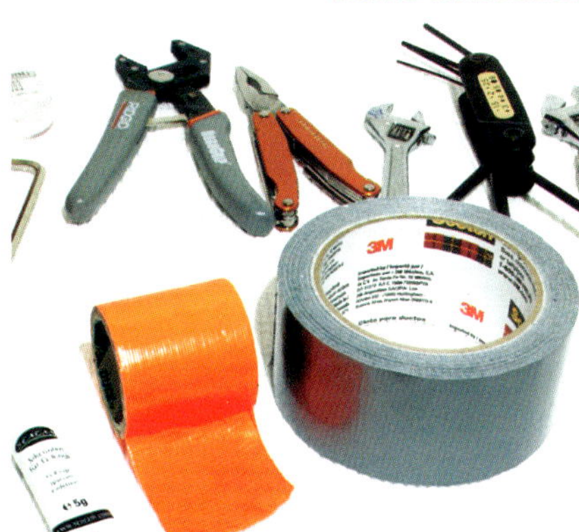

**Duct tape
- life saver for
photographers
- never leave
home without it!**

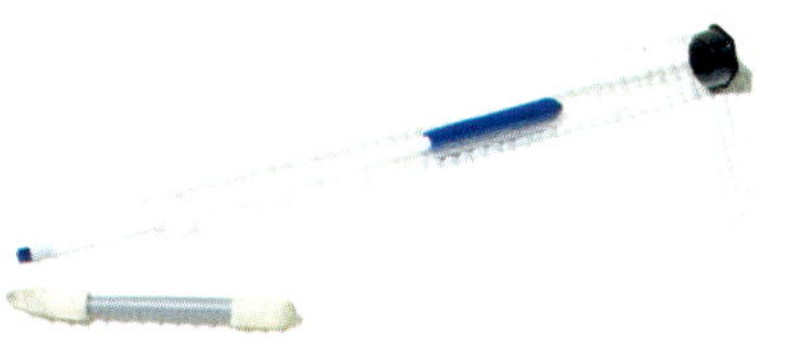

*Make-up applicator and static dust
remover – additional essentials for
a digital photographer's tool kit.*

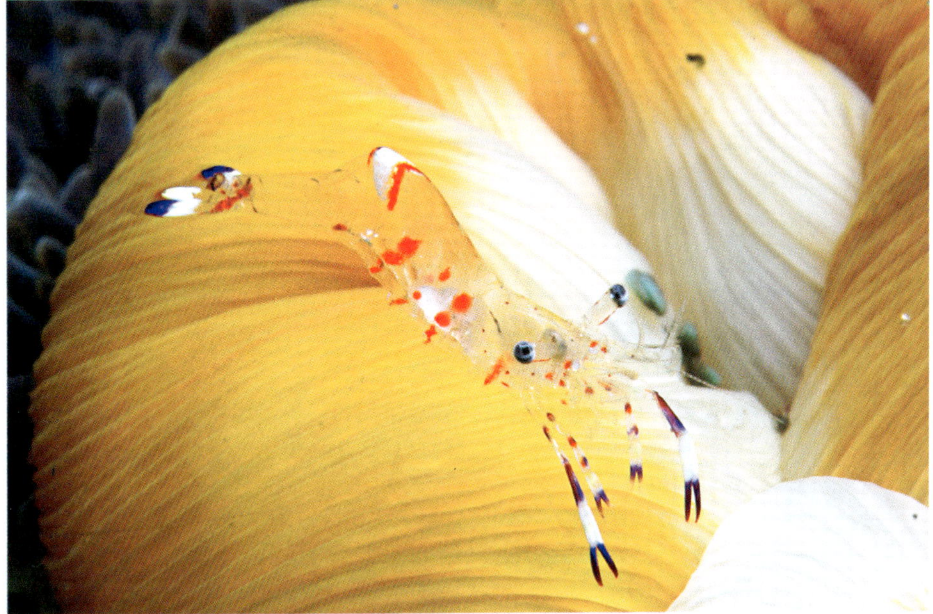

*Pericliminus shrimp with host anemone.
Bethlehem, Manado, 2005.
Nikon D2X, Seacam housing: f32, 1/60sec, -0.3EV, Single Ikelite S200 1/2 power*

Module TWO
Shooting Digital Underwater

2/1 Seeing Colour & Light Underwater

Lighting conditions underwater differ significantly to those on land. Mastering the use and control of light is the essence of successful Photography.

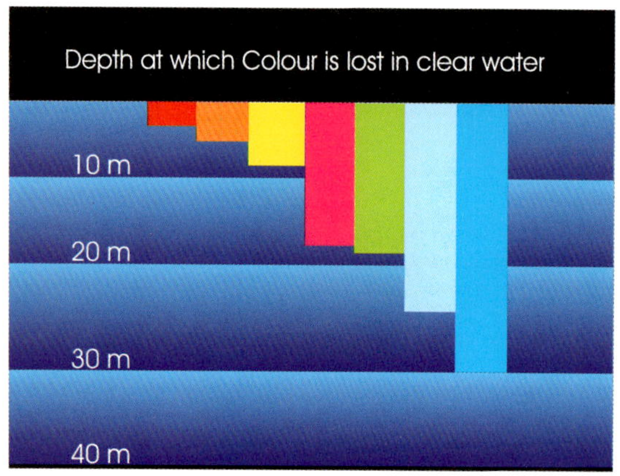

3 metres red is gone.
5 metres orange is gone.
10 metres yellow is gone.
18 metres green is gone.
25 metres blue green is gone.
30 metres only blue remains.

Colour and Light Underwater

As a scuba diver you would have learnt that colour diminishes with depth; water particles interact with light by absorbing respective wave lengths (see diagram). First the reds and oranges disappear, followed by yellows, greens and purples and lastly the blue. The loss of the colour red is dramatic as it is already noticeable at just one metre depth. Another factor that challenges an underwater photographer is that light also diminishes with depth. The density of water being 800 times denser than air at sea level reduces sunlight penetration.

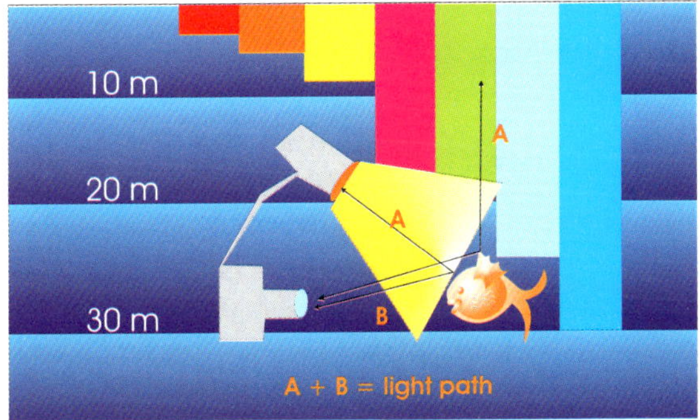

Horizontal distance also reduces light. If you are three metres deep and three metres from the subject, the water between you and the subject absorbs red and orange light as though you were about six metres deep. Compounding the two factors; photographs captured at beyond 10 metres are mostly blue and green. The ocean absorbs the long wave length light (the red end of spectrum) first. Short wave length light (the blue end of spectrum) is absorbed last.

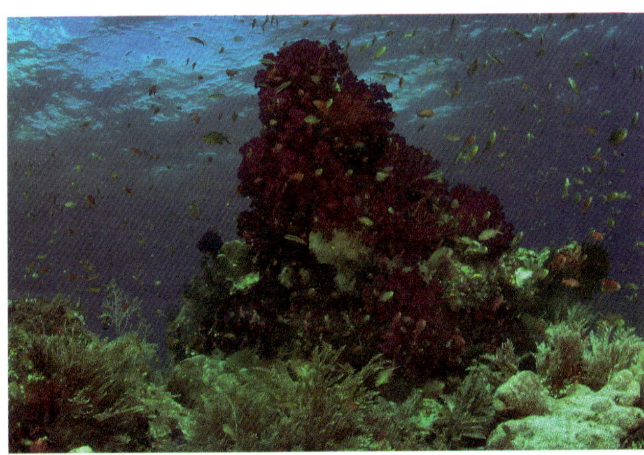

Shot at 15m natural light - note the blue tinge - loss of red, orange, yellow.

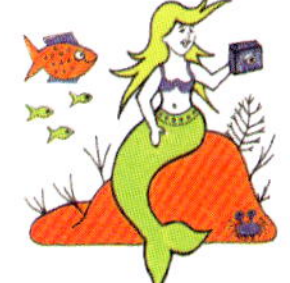

HINTS

1. Natural light photography deeper than six metres will have a bluish tinge.

2. A UR-PRO filter can be used to artificially restore some of the colour, at the sacrifice of one f-stop. But in bright daylight the UR-PRO filter will cause a strong orange tinge when used in water shallower than six metres.

3. Alternative light sources such as underwater strobes are absolutely essential to capture the 'true' colour of marine animals.

Seeing the light - naturally

To create beautiful underwater pictures, you need to be able to appreciate natural light. Seeing light in the aqueous realm begins with an understanding of how water is affected by light from the sun and flash. Most underwater photos are illuminated in some way by strobes, which bring out the vibrant colours associated with marine animals. All successful photographers are expert with use of ambient light. Most seascape imagery lends itself to use of natural light and wide-angle images rely on the background being illuminated by the sun.

A good use of the sun's position has a critical effect on the result achieved when shooting with natural light. If the sun's light is coming from your back, your subject will be well illuminated and appear light against a dark deep blue background. The idea is to be as close as possible to your subject to prevent any shades of blue (or green) from merging with those of the background. The idea is get close – get rid of the water.

Another dramatic art form of underwater photography is silhouetted images. This is achieved when a subject is placed in front of the sun. The subject's black form is then silhouetted against a pleasant blue (or green) background or sunburst. With careful execution, dramatic images can be easily achieved with digital cameras. The morning sun between 9am to 11am is the best time to shoot natural light.

HOW to Shoot with Natural Light

1. Best to have sun behind you to light up subject in front of you.

2. Try by placing subject between lens and the sun, to achieve a spectacular silhouette with the sun's rays radiating from around it. Best to shoot in Shutter Priority at a shutter speed of 1/125s or more to freeze these dramatic sunrays, also known as cathedral lights.

3. Use portrait orientation to maximise the use of the water column. The water column is much brighter and ideal for silhouette shots large subjects - wrecks, mantas, coral trees.

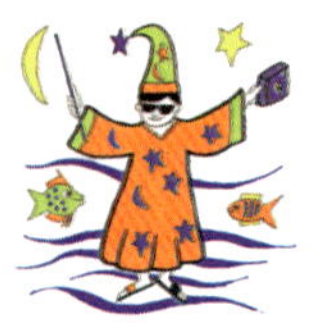

moire effect - result of pointing directly at the sun

CRITICAL NOTE: Even the most expensive DSLR cameras do not handle sunbursts as well as traditional film. Avoid pointing straight into the sun – but point into the water column at a slight skyward angle.

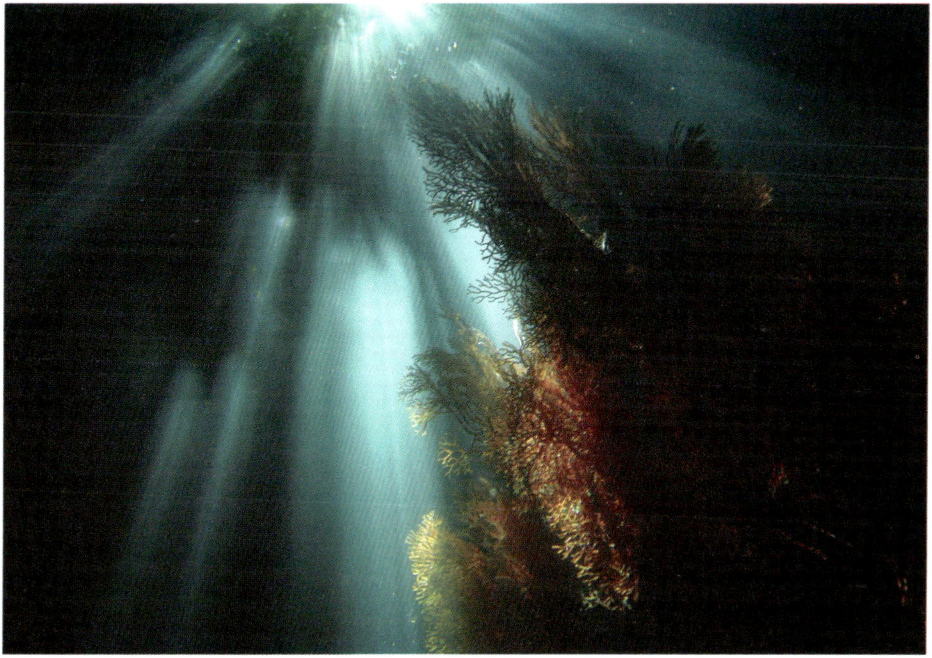

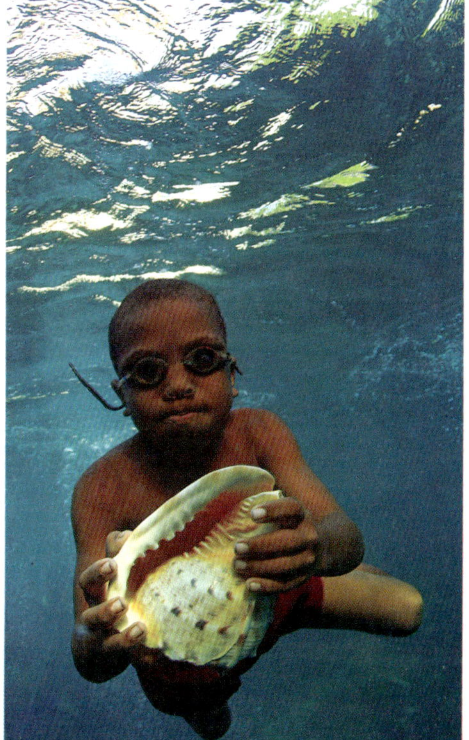

'Cathedral in the Passage'
Raja Ampat
SONY 828 - natural light
f5, 1/125s, -0.7 EV. Ikelite housing

Shooting with natural light is perhaps the simplest form of underwater imagery and, if treated artistically, the results beautifully reveal the mysteries of the sea.

'Dancing with the Shell'
Kri Island, Raja Ampat
Nikon D100, 16mm 2.8 lens
natural light
f5, 1/160s, -1 EV. AQUATICA housing

Criteria for selecting STROBES

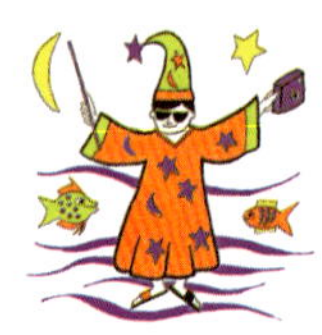

1. Make sure that the strobe is compatible with your housing, i.e. do not purchase a strobe which attaches to the camera with a sync cord if your housing does not have a bulkhead.

2. Prosumer camera users - make sure the strobe incorporates a pre-flash cancellation function if you are using a fibre optic cable to make the link with the digital camera. This is not a problem when choosing Ikelite.

3. Check the Power rating – this is typically expressed in terms of guide number. This number is directly proportional to the power of the strobe The higher the number, the more powerful the strobe.

4. Power Selection – a good strobe will as a minimum give options to power down to 1/2, 1/4, 1/8, plus the option for TTL. Of course, there's always the option to purchase an Ikelite Slave manual dialler that allows 10 power down options.

5. Angle of Coverage: this should be in relation to the angle covered by your camera lens. The angle of coverage of the strobe should ideally be greater or equal to that of your lens in order to avoid darker zones at the periphery of the picture. For example, if you are using a 16mm wide angle lens, your strobe should have a minimum of 90º angle of coverage.

6. One of the prime considerations when choosing a strobe is the recycle time – many good shots are missed because of recycle time. The difference in recycle times between a fast and a slow recycling strobe may make the difference between getting and missing that perfect shot. As an illustration of this, the Ikelite DS125 recycles in 1 second after a full power dump, compared to more than 5 seconds for other digital strobes. Anything more than a 1 second is not ideal.

7. Shooting Stamina - the number of shots you can get with a fully charged battery is crucial. You don't want to go out for a multi dive day, only to find out that your strobe battery dies the first dive. Choose a strobe that gives at least 120 flashes at full power with a fully-charged battery.

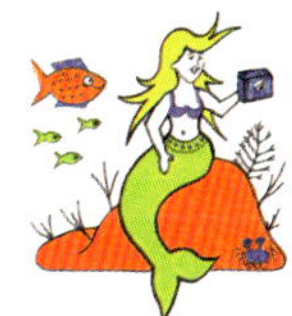

HINT – get a strobe with multi power settings, that recycles in 1 second or less at full power, and uses a rechargeable battery pack that gives more than 120 flashes per charge.

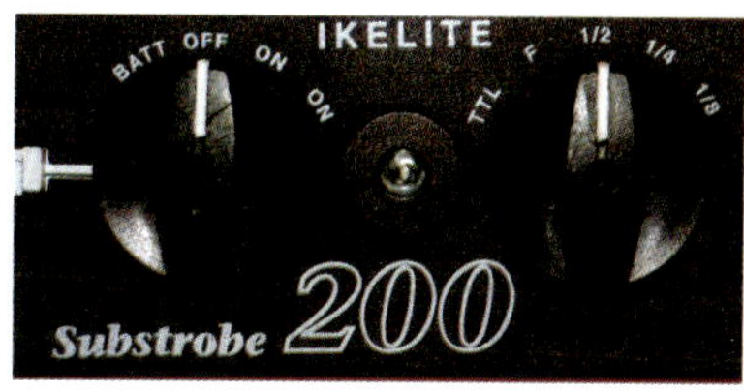

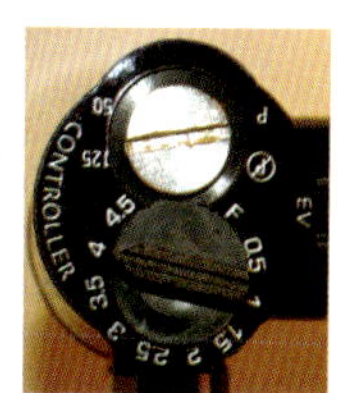

The Ikelite Manual power setting slave controller with multi setting is a great device for manual strobe exposure.

Deeper into Strobes

Most of the consumer underwater housings do not allow a direct connection of an external strobe to the camera. This simple fact implies that, in most cases, there needs to be some form of indirect link between the camera and the strobe. This is typically achieved by using "slave" strobe: the internal flash of the digital camera is used to trigger the external strobe. Another issue that arises from the use of digital cameras with external strobe is the inherent pre-flash function used for topside flash photography. Pre-flash does not work for underwater photography.

Solutions for Prosumer users

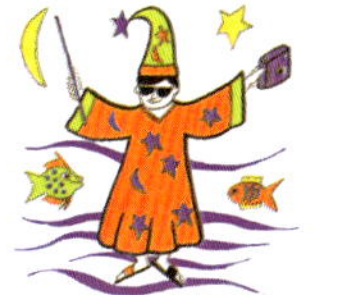

How to use a Fibre Optic Link

1. Disable the pre-flash function.
2. Mask the internal flash of the camera with duct tape or equivalent. This also prevents backscatter.
3. Link to the strobe is made using a fibre optic cable that is attached to the strobe at one end, and to the camera, through the black patch, at the other end. Strobes that use this type of configuration include the Epoque ES-150DS, and Inon D-180 and Z220/S digital strobes.

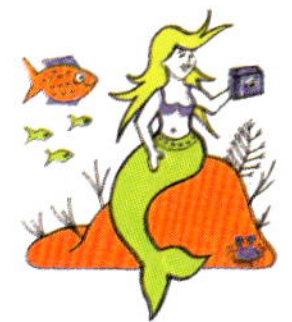

HINTS

1. This sort of link works best when camera is used in Manual mode (with the built-in flash covered, automatic settings may not work correctly).
2. Fibre optic cables are relatively fragile, are prone to breaking and can be become dislodged. Care should be taken during setting up and handling to avoid damage or dislodging of the cable. Although they are relatively inexpensive, they are the weakest link and could result in many lost photo opportunities.

How to use a Slave Sensor

1. Connect the sensor to the strobe.

2. Mask the front section of the housing around the area where the built in flash of the camera face with duct tape or equivalent. This also prevents backscatter.

3. Face the sensor towards the top of the camera housing – this link only works with a clear Perspex housing.

4. When the camera is triggered, the sensor then watches what the camera flash does, and in turn instructs the strobe to flash at the same intensity. Thus when the camera emits a pre-flash followed by the actual flash, the strobe does the same. This method has the advantage of working better than the previous one when the camera is used in Automatic mode. The strobes that use this device are currently only produced by Ikelite.

5. The slave sensor will quench the external strobe, instructing it to stop emitting light at the same time as the internal flash. Attach an Ikelite manual controller and you will be able to adjust the intensity of the flash.

Dedicated Sync cord

This is by far the most reliable method. This is by use of a sync cord to link up your strobe directly to the camera. This is the best all round solution, but is only possible if you are using high-end prosumer or DSLR camera housing that incorporates a bulkhead for connecting the sync cord. The options available include: Ikelite, Seacam and Aquatica housings for Sony, Olympus, Nikon and Canon cameras.

Vital NOTE: the bulkhead on the strobe and housing are the vital link for the strobe to talk to the housing. Align the sync cord precisely as per instructions provided by the housing / strobe manufacturer. Most strobes use the Nikonos fitting (apart from Ikelite and Sea&Sea). Even though it is the most popular system, its design is inherently prone to flooding. The threads on the bulkhead are internal making them little traps for water and dirt. Over time, even the most prudent user will one day discover a flooded bulkhead. To avoid this problem convert sync cord and bulkheads to the Ikelite type, for which the threads of the bulkhead are on the outside.

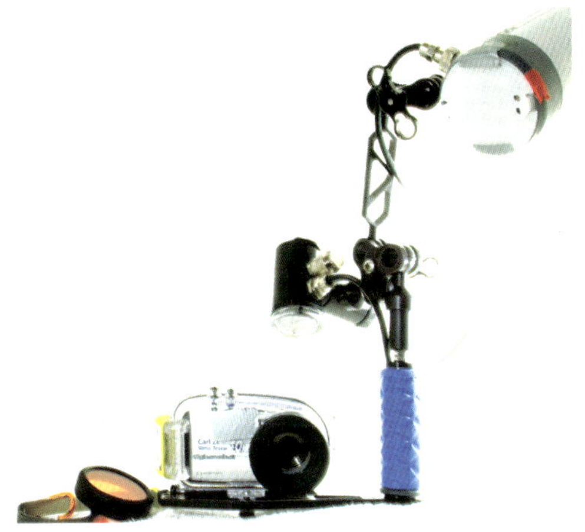

Ikelite DS50 strobe mounted with Ultralight arms / sensor is pointed at back of housing and note that the internal flash is masked.

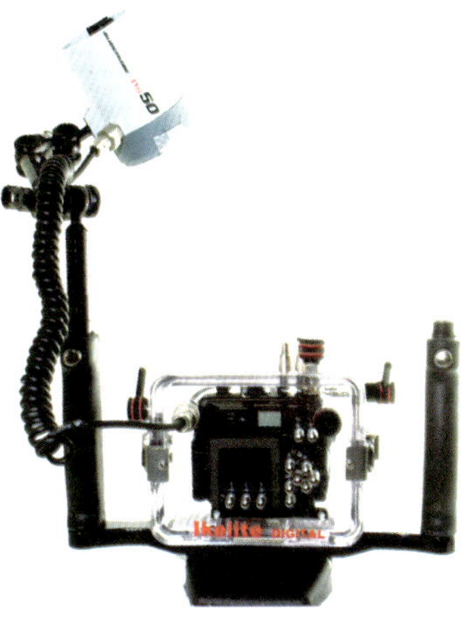

Ikelite DS50 strobe mounted with Ultralight arms and connected to back of housing with a sync chord.

Positioning Strobes

Good placement of artificial light is a very important element in well exposed images. Arms for your strobe are like an extension of your own – they should be rigid yet flexible and responsive.

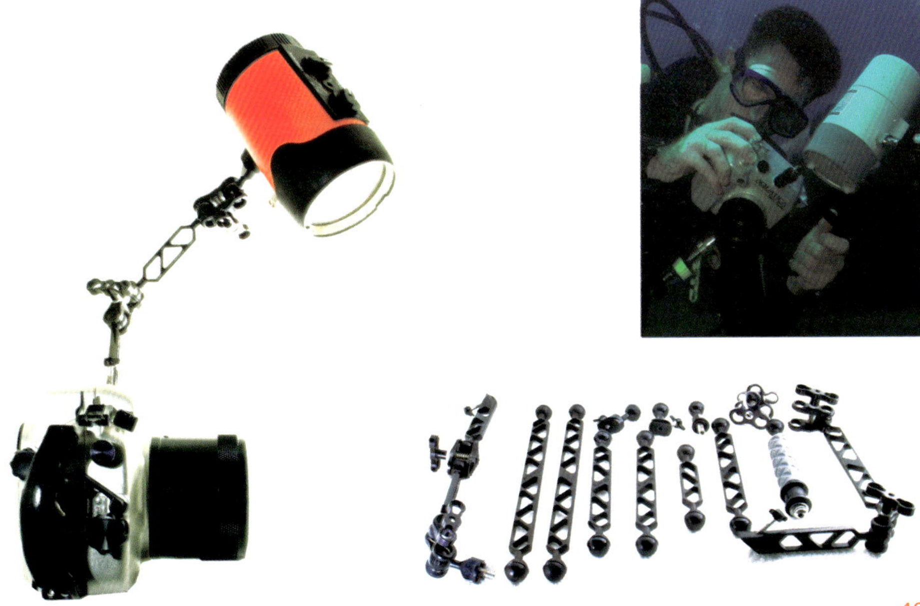

2/3 Strobe Orientation and Positioning

Understanding Backscatter

Backscatter is generated when the light from strobe hits tiny particles and bounces back towards the lens. This refraction process can be horribly magnified. This effect is compounded with particles that are outside the area of the subject in focus (e.g. in front of the main subject). This in turn makes the refracted particles blurred, and appearing even larger.

Backscatter essentially makes an otherwise great picture horrifying! Most annoying, these 'snow storms' are rarely visible at the moment that we are actually taking the photo. One of the key issues when using strobes is orientating them in such a way to avoid or minimise backscatter. Even in very clear water, there are always fine particles (e.g. sand or silt) or micro-organisms (plankton) which could potentially result in backscatter. There are a few approaches to avoid or reduce this devastating effect.

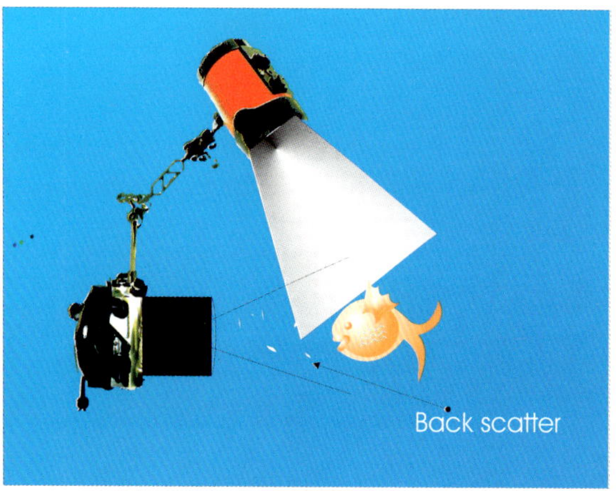

To minimise backscatter: angle strobe to light up subject and not the area in front of lens - GET CLOSER

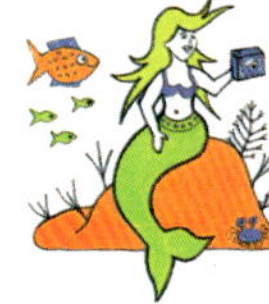

HINTS

1. The best way of getting the strobe away from the housing is hand holding the strobe. This method offers the greatest flexibility, as adjustments come naturally.

2. A less cumbersome and effective solution is to use purpose-made arms which attach to the housing at one end, and to the strobe at the other end. These allow for easy positioning of the strobe, without the need to permanently hold the latter – the Ultra-light arms system is often used.

3. Fire a few shots to determine where light falls over the subject. Adjust accordingly.

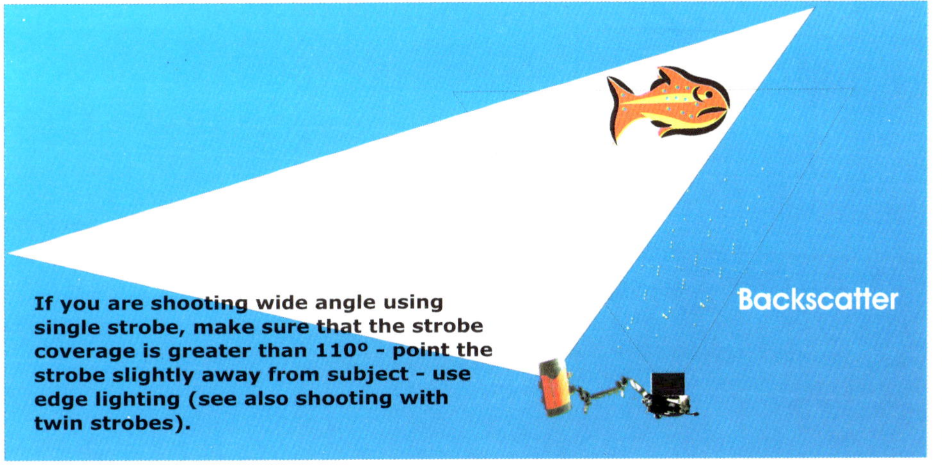

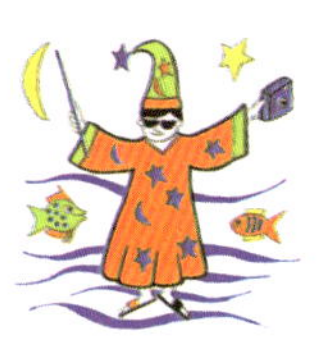

How to avoid Backscatter

1. Orientate strobes at an angle away from the subject - see above illustration. This will light up the subject and minimise lighting up scatters.

2. If you must point the strobe at the subject, pull the strobe as far away or to the side as possible from the camera. This has the additional advantage of lighting up a smaller zone in front of the subject than if the strobe were closer to the camera. This in itself contributes to reducing backscatter, as particles located behind the subject are further away from the strobe.

3. For macro, you may consider using a continuous light instead of strobe light and longer shutter speeds of between 0.1 and 1 seconds. A 50 watt Treble-light HID or other HMI lights are a good option in dirty water. This method has given stunning results in murky water with less than one metre visibility but it requires a steady tripod, still subjects and some experience.

4. Generally speaking, you need to have very good buoyancy control for underwater photography. Amongst other things, good buoyancy control helps avoid stirring up the bottom when taking shots, which will invariably lead to backscatter. If you need to brush up on your buoyancy skills, ask your dive instructor. There are numerous programs available to help you improve.

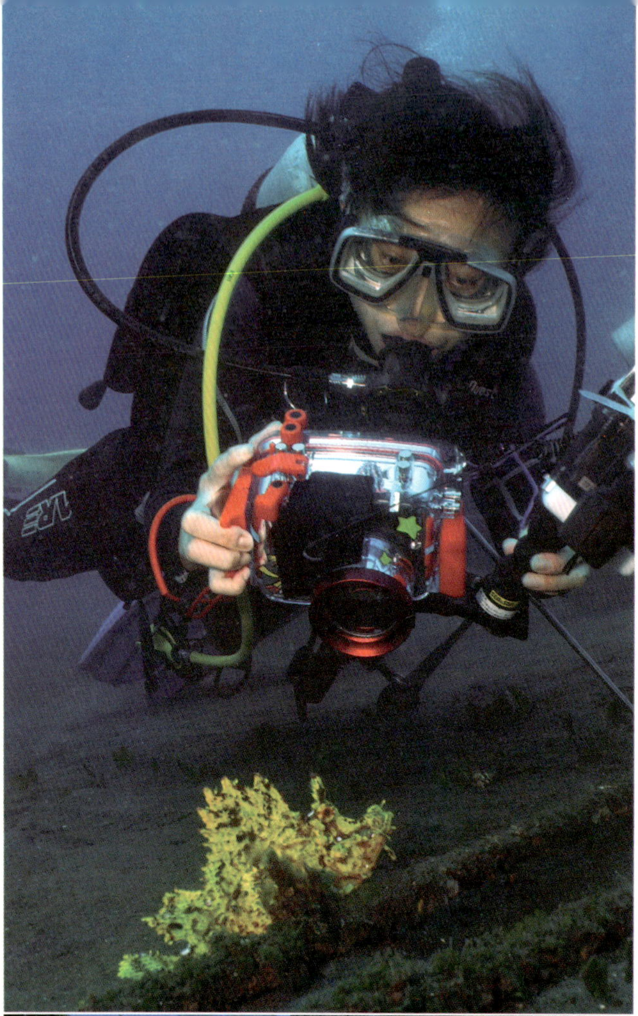

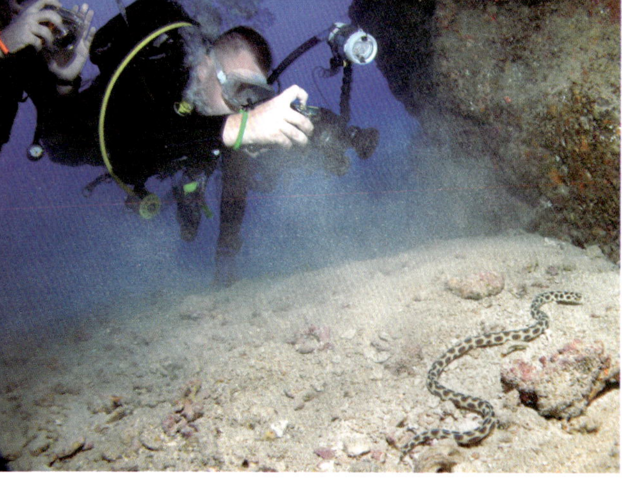

Good buoyancy, angled strobe placement & getting close equals good pictures.

Bad buoyancy & bad strobe placement equals bad picture.

DIFFUSERS

Diffusers are translucent plastic covers that can be attached to the front of strobes. Diffusers have several interesting properties. First of all, they obviously diffuse the light coming from the strobe. Some strobes exhibit a "hot spot" in the centre of the beam, and softer light at the perimeter of the beam. Diffusers help alleviate this issue by spreading the light from the strobe more evenly.

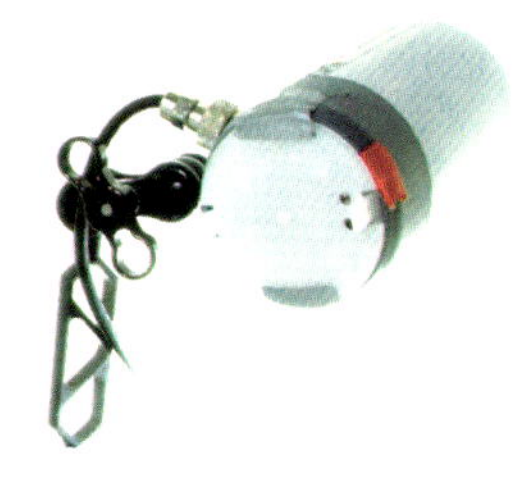

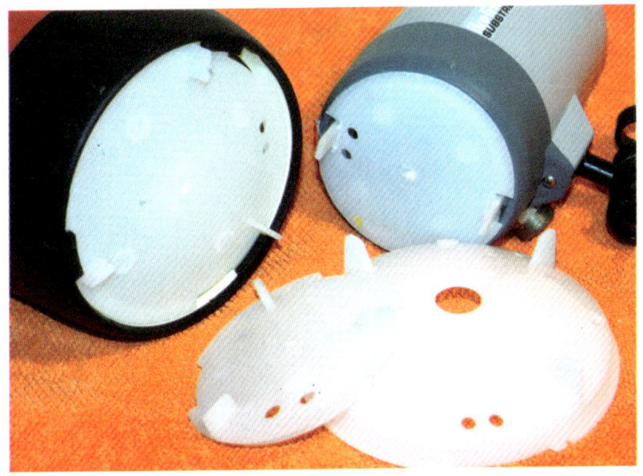

Because diffusers are translucent, they also tend to absorb part of the light emitted by the strobe. This can be useful when the strobe is too powerful, even when set at its lowest setting. This technique is particularly helpful when taking macro or close-focus wide-angle shots. Finally, diffusers spread the light from the strobe in such a way that it covers a greater area. This is particularly helpful when shooting with wide-angle or fisheye lenses. With such lenses, which can "see" a very large area, the strobe will most likely not be able to light up the entire scene without using diffusers.

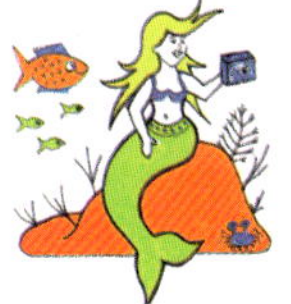

HINTS

1. Good strobe manufacturers also supply customised diffusers – get one. They are invaluable for wide angle photography.

2. When in the field, a white plastic bag or piece of white Perspex is a temporary fix.

3. If there isn't already one, make a small hole at the edge of your diffuser, and use it to tie a small cord and attach it to your strobe. They do tend to have a habit of swimming away.

2/4 Playing with Light

In addition to proper positioning and orientation of your strobes, the total amount of light reaching your subject will have a tremendous impact on your pictures. If the light is too strong or too weak, your picture will be overexposed or underexposed, and details will be lost. It's all about playing with light and striking the right balance.

Appreciating Underexposed Images:

Inadequate light (aperture too small, or shutter speed too fast) can at times enhance contrast. Generally an underexposed image is easier to correct than an overexposed one. Some photographers deliberately underexpose their images by 1/2 stop to obtain better details and contrast (this image is shot at -1 EV to show the intricacies of the reef).

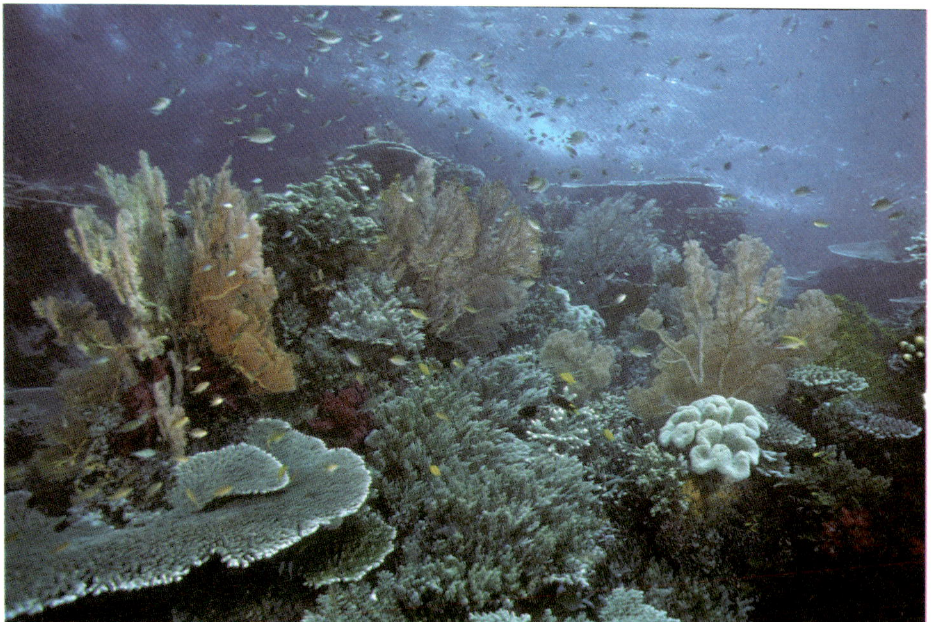

Mike Point - Raja Ampat
Nikon D100, Seacam housing. Twin Ikelite S200 strobe, 1/2 power
14mm 2.8 lens, f8, 1/60sec, ISO 160 EV-1

Balancing Strobe & Natural Light

One of the most popular techniques consists of balancing the artificial light from the strobe with the natural light from the sun. This works best with wide-angle shots, when you have both the subject illuminated by the strobes in the foreground, and the water lit up by the sun in the background.

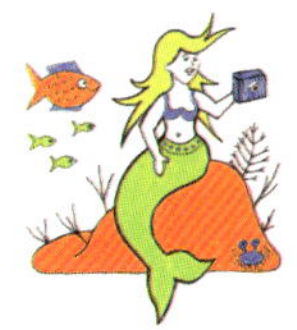

How to SHOOT Wide Angle Balanced Light

1. The starting point for all balanced light shots is an ambient light reading. Decide the direction of camera angle – where are you going to point your camera? Into or away from the sun, skyward or straight ahead?

2. Take a light reading of the background by half-pressing the shutter release, set your aperture according to that reading. Typically, midday in 10 metres of water the setting is f/8.

3. Use Aperture Priority or Manual mode – set shutter speed to 1/60s.

4. Adjust strobe power to the distance between strobes and the subject – generally I will start with 1/2 power.

5. If your strobes do not have a power setting knob, you'll have to adjust its distance to the subject by moving it closer or further away.

6. If your system is capable of handling TTL, then simply choose the TTL setting on your strobe. TTL works better with a -1 EV compensation.

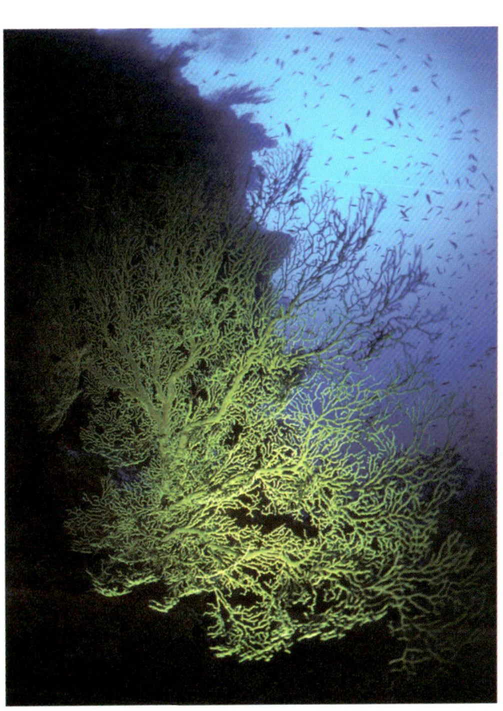

7. Trigger and review your shot. Adjust and shoot again.

HINTS

An interesting scenario is shooting fish with shiny skin. The high reflectivity of the fish will invariably cause overexposed subjects and lost detail, which at best can be distracting and at worst ruin the shot completely. When shooting a school of barracudas or jacks, play with the lighting in the following manner:
1. decrease exposure by -1EV; if you are already on -1, set to -2 and/or
2. decrease strobe setting by 1/2 stop.

Close Focus Wide Angle (CFWA) Balanced Light

Here it is once again – get in close and personal – it is the only way to create dramatic perspectives and sharp pictures. The great advantage of shooting close focus wide-angle lens is that it will divide the frame into a dominant foreground and a scenic backdrop. Of course, with less water between the lens and subject, the colour reproduction will also be much better on your final image. Generally at wide-angle range, the depth-of-field is much greater, thus it is unnecessary to use small apertures. Larger apertures (f/8, f/5.6) bring more ambient light onto your sensor.

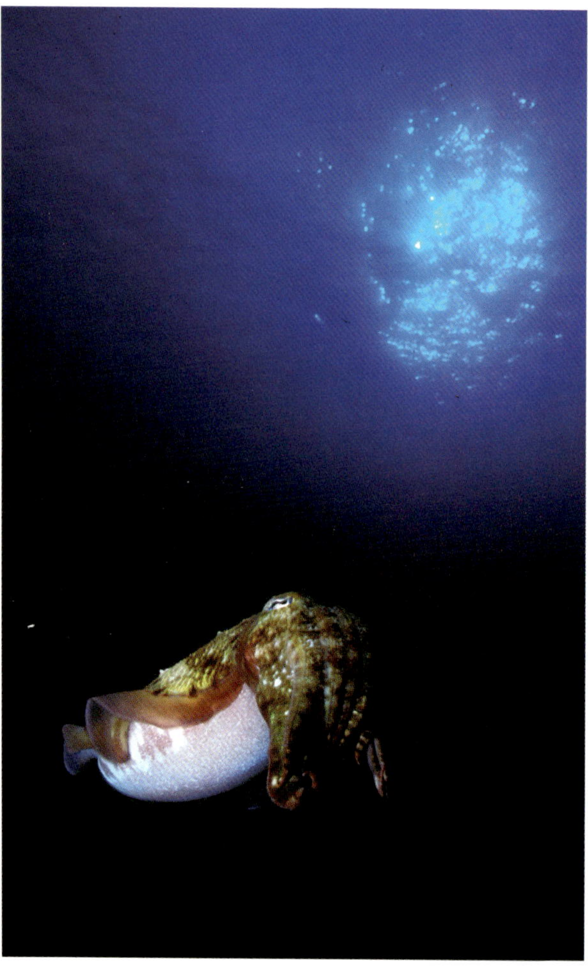

Richelieu Rock, Thailand
Nikon D1X, Seacam housing, single Ikelite
S200 @ 1/2 power, f11, 1/60sec, ISO 200.

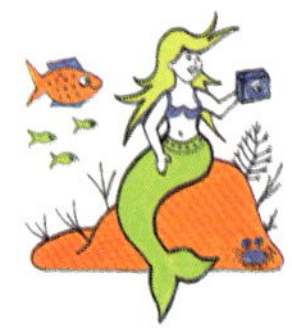

HINTS

• For close up subjects, sharp focus is absolutely critical. Use a shutter speed of at least 1/30s.

• For CFWA, it is possible to greatly expand the depth-of-field by closing down the aperture. It is not uncommon to shoot CFWA at f/22 in clear, bright conditions. The strobe will provide adequate illumination for this distance.

• Shooting with a large depth-of-field may produce dramatic results.

• Strobe should be held to the side of the housing to reduce backscatter. Of course, the closer you get to your subject, the less water, the fewer particles, and therefore the less chance for backscatter.

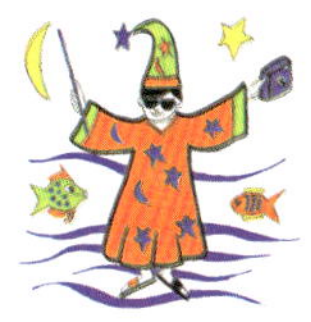

How to Shoot Close Focus Wide Angle (CFWA)

1. Choose your close-up subject and position yourself accordingly – normally between 20 to 30 cm away (Giant frogfish, feather stars, cuttlefish, sponges are all ideal).

2. As with wide angle, starting point for CFWA is ambient light reading.

3. Decide on camera angle and point accordingly.

4. Take a light reading of the background by half-pressing the shutter release, set your aperture according to that reading.

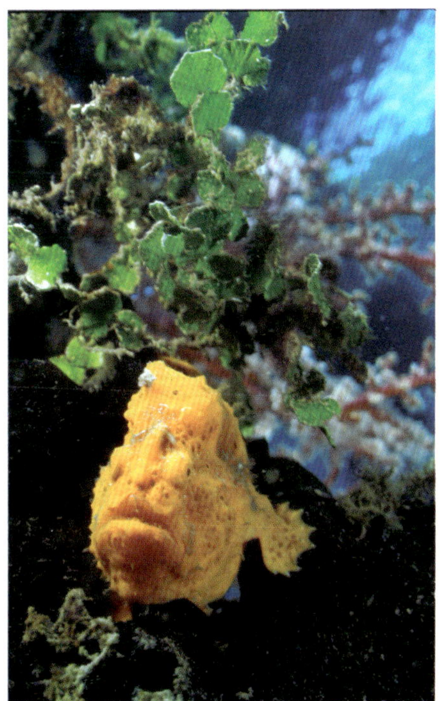

5. Use Manual mode - set shutter speed to 1/125 sec.

6. TTL may not work - if the subject is just 30 centimetres away from the camera and flashgun, it could well be overexposed since a TTL flashgun might not be able to quench its flash fast enough.

7. Shoot and preview - bracket with strobe setting or strobe distance.

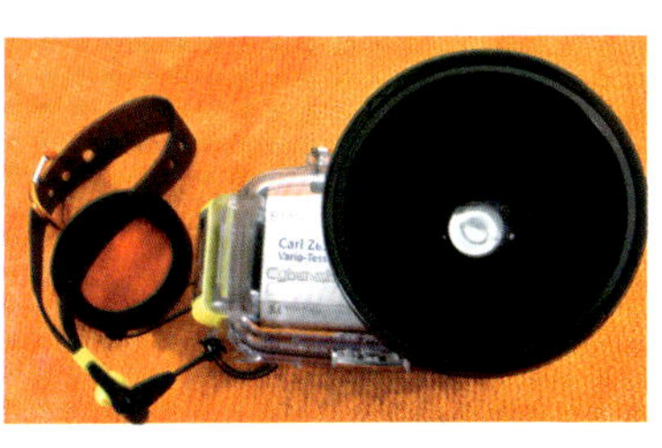
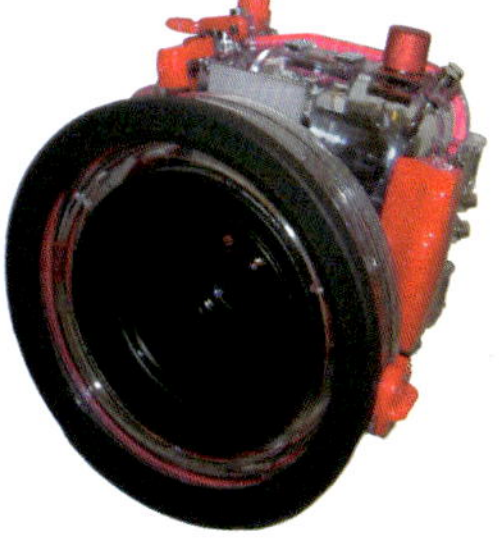

Some Consumer/Prosumer cameras are supported by a range of wide angle lenses. Check if the housing is supported before purchase.

How to Shoot Macro with an External Flash

Macro imagery is perhaps one of the most rewarding forms of underwater photography. It has the quickest learning curve and is the easiest to master. Extreme close-up photography often produces stunning portraits of minute critters, as well as creative renderings of composition not possible with standard or wide-angle lenses.

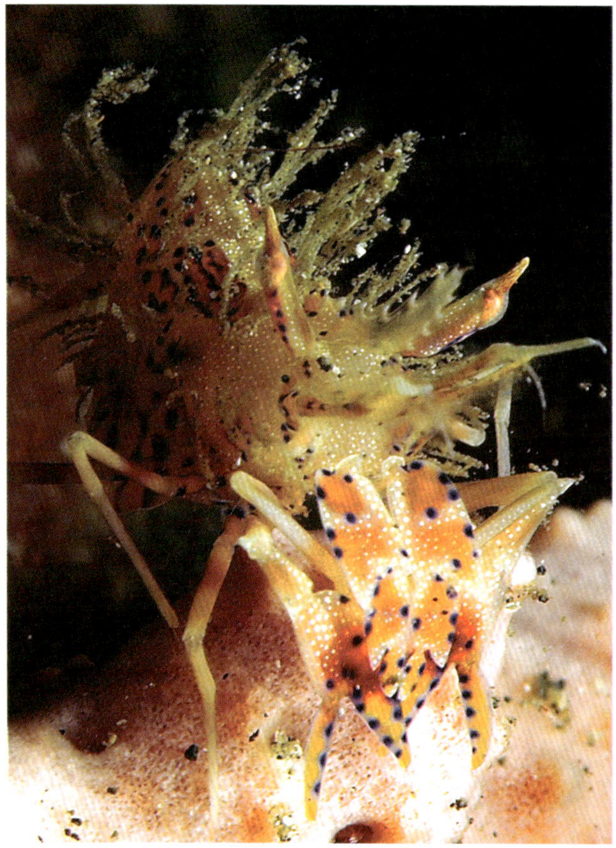

Tiger shrimp -
Lembeh Strait
Nikon D1X, Seacam housing, Ikelite S200 strobe 1/2 power f32, 1/60 sec

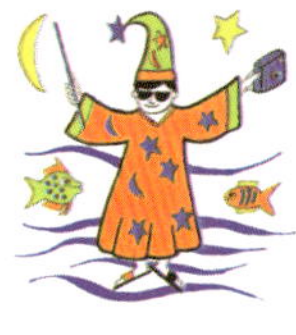

HOW TO SHOOT MACRO

1. Set ISO dial to the lowest (e.g. 64 or 100).

2. Set the shutter speed dial to A for TTL automatic flash or 1/60th second for manual flash mode.

3. Set the lens aperture to the smallest aperture (f/22 for DSLR or f/8 for Con/Prosumer). This is done to gain maximum possible depth of field.

4. Set the strobe on TTL or smallest setting for manual control.

5. Aim strobe at a 45º angle pointing down towards the subject.

6. Adjust strobe distance to subject according to the manufacturer's recommendation (Guide Number) for the strobe you are using.

7. Review with LCD and bracket down or up using strobe power or aperture.

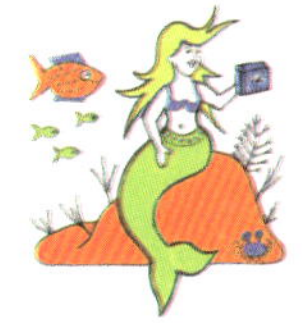

HINTS

• For a black background, position camera angle at the same plane towards the subject with water in the background.

• For a blue background aim the camera slightly up towards the surface, balance ambient lighting by reducing the shutter speed to 1/30s or opening up the aperture to f/5.6, and decreasing strobe power or pulling the flash unit further away from the subject.

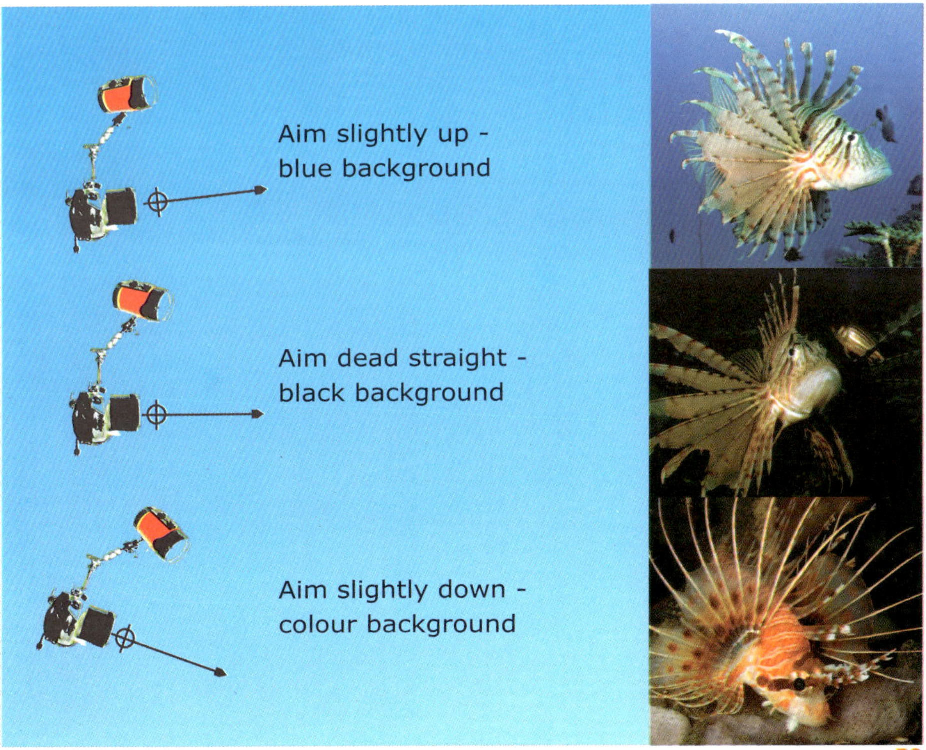

The Rembrandt Technique – Single Directional Light Source

This technique is adapted from methods used in the advertising industry. To create the illusion of the third dimension, glamour photographers use the Rembrandt lighting technique to achieve an aura and add impact to their portrait. It is no big secret. As photographers, we should be cognisant of light and shadows, especially on how these elements interact around subjects. It is how we "see" the light as well as the shadows.

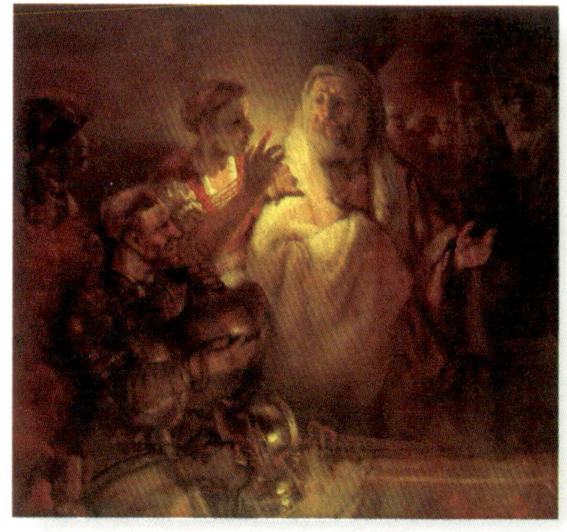

This technique was first employed by the old master – Rembrandt. His single light source is his signature, defining the style of his masterpieces. Continuing into the present day, many successful modern portrait artists are familiar with this style, and are adept at this classic lighting technique. Combined with the three-quarter view of the face, this lighting creates a very flattering effect (especially for women), slimming down the face and highlighting the cheeks. This highlighting of the "broad" side of the face is a hallmark of "Rembrandt" lighting.

Though he worked mostly with subjects in the nude, I am sure Rembrandt would be impressed that I have borrowed his technique mostly for fish portraits. Of course, we can also use it to shoot glamour underwater, but that would not be much of a challenge.

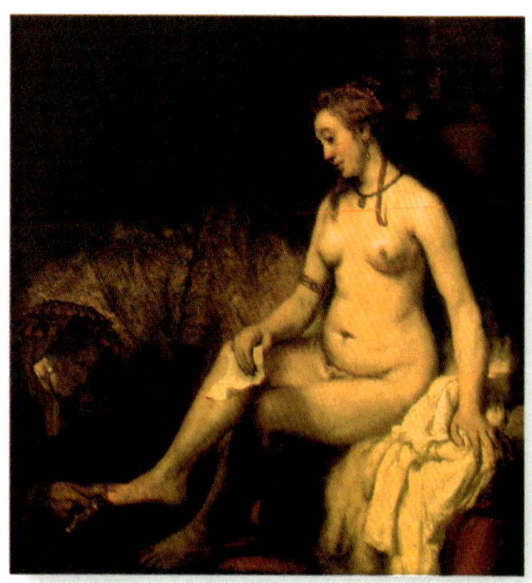

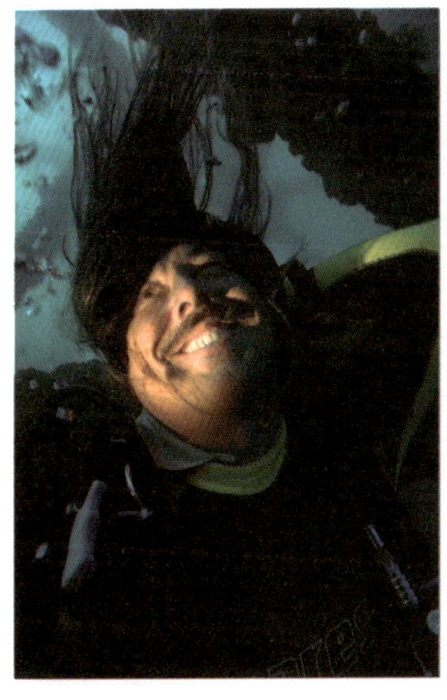

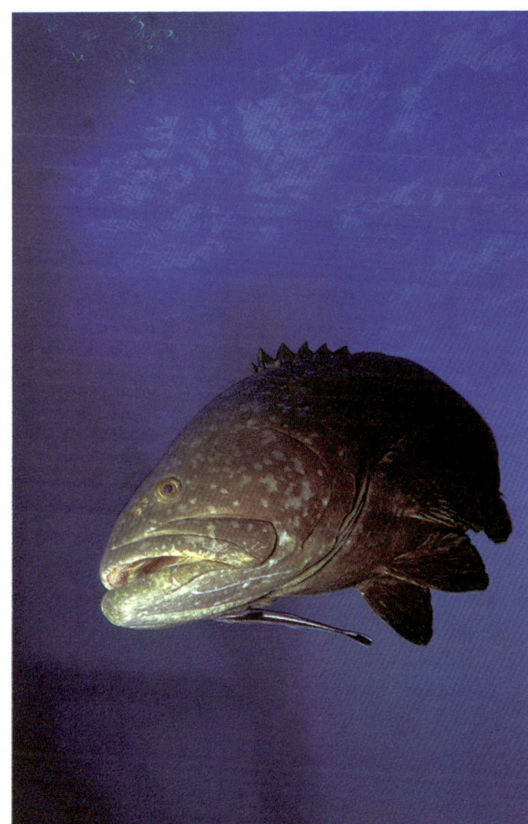

Primarily, the technique uses only one light source, angled at 45º from the left or right to light up one side of the subject. By using a snoot or a honeycomb diffuser, you can spread your modelling light, casting a gentler shadow on the other side. The degree of pronouncement of this triangular patch of light can be adjusted by the intensity and angle of the light, as well as the positioning of the face.

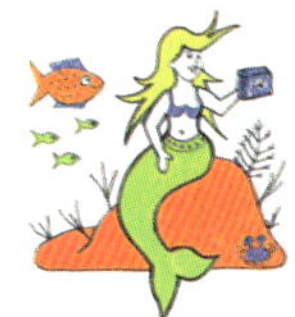

HINT

As the technique suggests, this a fine art form of lighting. Use it prudently to achieve a pleasing result.

While we can't really tell our subjects to turn 45º to their side, we can certainly reposition ourselves or our light to achieve the 'bright cheek' and the shadow on the other side.

Is ONE Strobe or TWO better?

The bottom line is, two strobes may not necessarily be better. Award-winning images are equally successfully captured with a single strobe. If you are starting out, it is best to explore the possibilities with using one strobe before progressing to dual strobes. Numerous renowned underwater photographers shoot almost exclusively with one strobe. Many of the images in this book and in most coffee table pictorial books are captured with a single strobe.

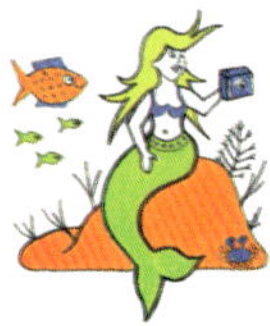

HINTS

1. Use a 2nd strobe when taking close-up shots of a bigger fish (hand to arm size) to reduce the harsh shadowing caused by only one light source.

2. Some wide-angle compositions demand the use of a second light to achieve a more balanced lighting and increase the area of light coverage. Lush seascapes, soft coral outcrops, etc. For wide-angle, make sure the strobes give at least 90º angle of coverage.

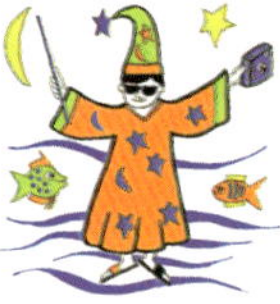

How to position two strobes for Macro

1. Portraits at extreme close range are best taken with two strobes.

2. Position each strobe to one side and above the subject so that the light falls at about 45º on the subject's face.

3. Power down the secondary strobe by one stop and position slightly further away from the subject. The brightness ratio between the strobes should be 2:1. This will produce soft shadows on one side of the animal's face and accentuate the other.

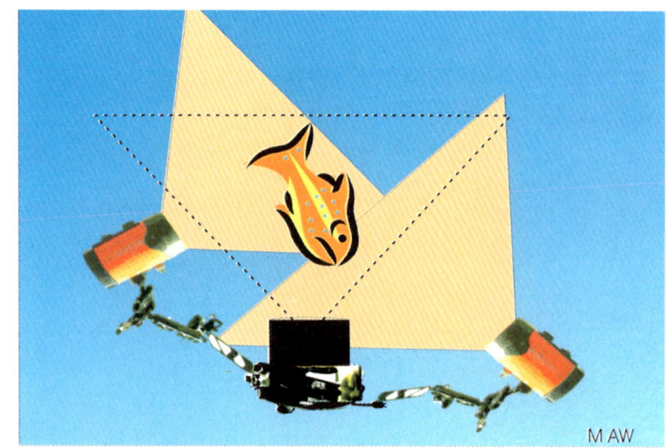

Using 2 strobes for macro

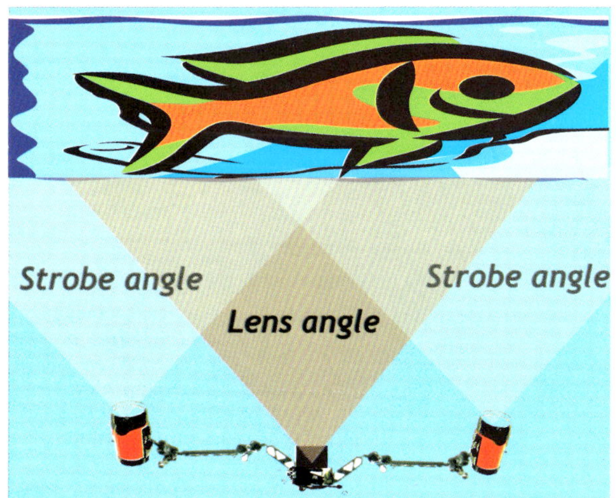

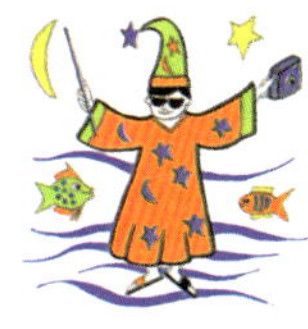

How to position two strobes for Wide Angle

1. The use of longer strobe arms is essential; position a strobe on each side of the housing and set them at a 45º angle, but face them slightly away from the subject. The objective is to use the edge of the each light to fall on the subject – also known as edge lighting. (see above figure)

2. TTL settings often don't work in these situations – set both strobes at half power as a starting point and bracket with strobe power for variation.

HINTS

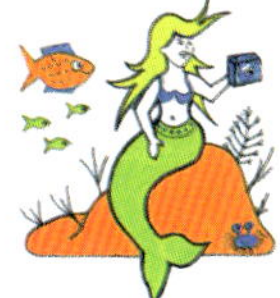

1. Move in close and bracket both exposure and your position.

2. Whilst the technical know-how is explained here, nothing beats experimenting and practice. The idea once again is to get rid of the water, and get in as close as you can. If the background is lit by natural light, use your strobe to add colour to the foreground subject producing a pleasing and atmospheric image.

Hot Wide-Angle tips from the Photo Wizard

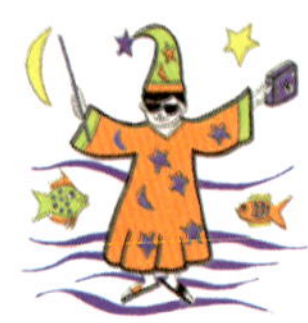

1. Identify a subject / composition that matches the width of your lens.

2. Consider the lighting for the image – will it be provided either by the sun or strobe, or a combination of both?

3. Set exposure for the most dominant light source.

4. Frame the picture; move around the subject and try various camera angles viewed through the viewfinder or LCD screen.

5. If you plan to use your buddy as model, rehearse on land first.

6. Generally a portrait orientation image that includes the water column and the sun (or sun rays) complements most subjects and immediately sets the underwater scene. Those taken at a downward angle will generally be darker and lack colour.

7. Beware of an overpowering background that may dominate your intended subject; it should complement the scene.

8. When taking wide-angle photographs it is easy to concentrate on the main subject and allow clutter (such as divers' arms and legs or air bubbles) to creep into the background. To prevent this from happening check all four corners of the viewfinder before pressing the shutter. Choose your background carefully.

9. With wide-angle work, to ensure that at least one of your shots comes out well-exposed and composed, take a few frames using different apertures and strobe-to-subject distances.

10. Wide-angle is radically much harder than macro work. Review glossy underwater pictorial books. Look at other underwater photographers' work for ideas and inspiration. Emulate some of the pictures and recreate them in your own individual way. There is a lot of scope for individual style in wide-angle photography. It is by far the most difficult discipline in underwater imaging.

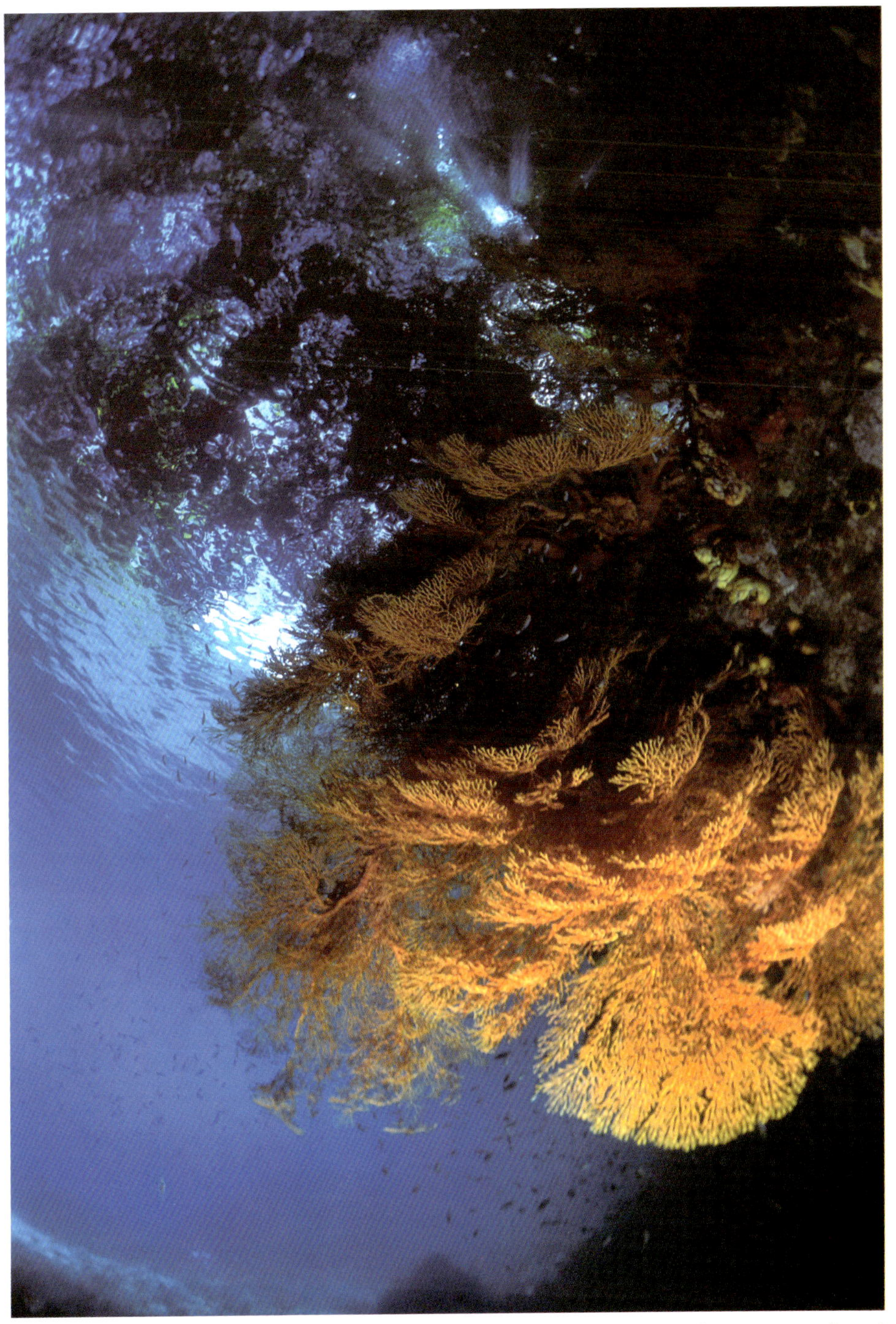

Seeing the Light - the ability to balance and use natural and artificial light is absolutely essential in wide angle images.

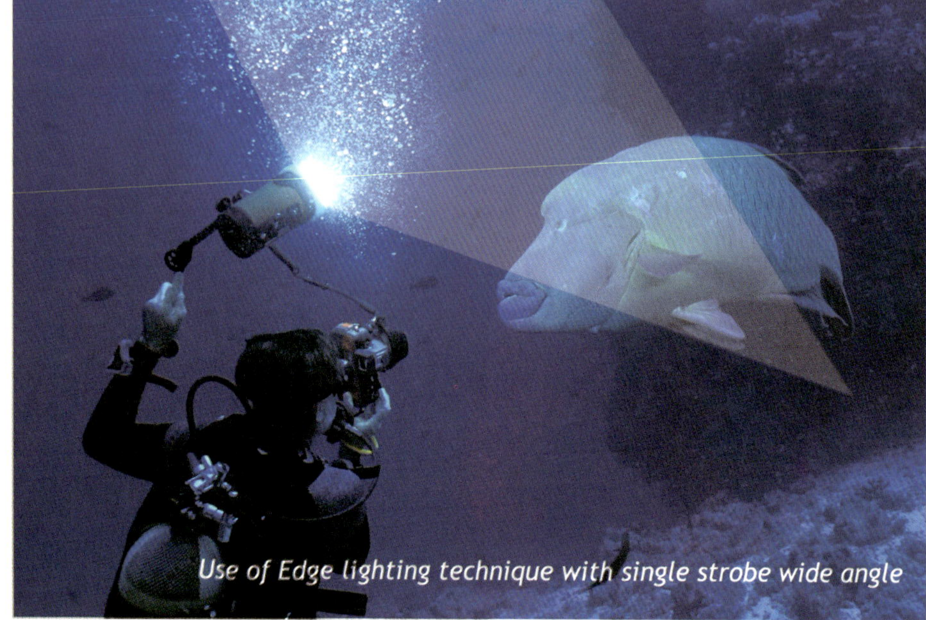

Stephen Frink - one of the world's most published underwater photographers using his best arm to edge light this friendly Napoleon wrasse in the Maldives. So here I am using a single Ikelite strobe to take a picture of him using a Ikelite S200 and somehow we managed to fire at the same time.

Three light sources contribute to this picture; the sun provided the top light and a single Ikelite S200 was used to light up the foreground. The powerful HID light hand held by the model adds to the interest of this plane wreck.

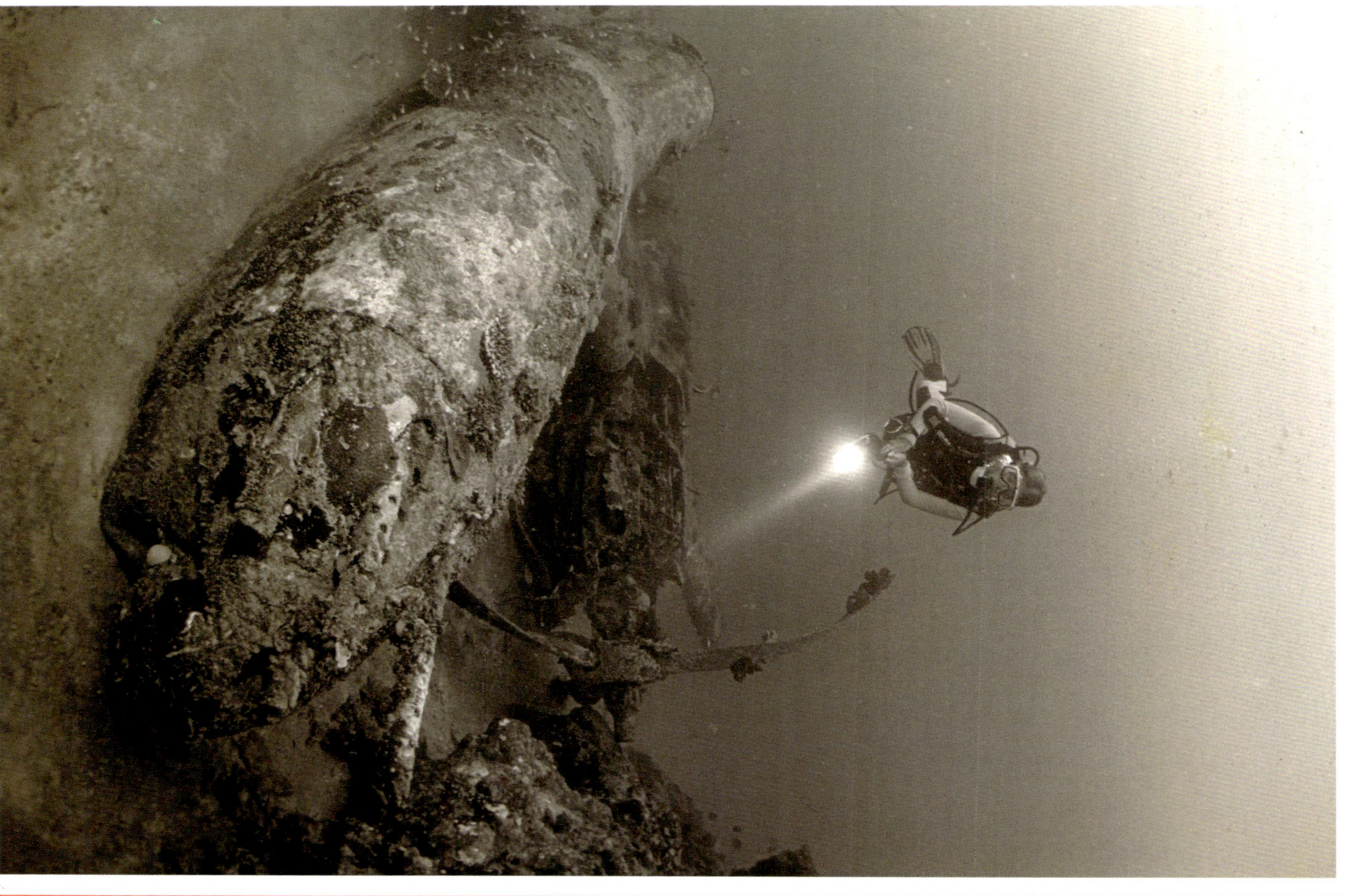

Module Three
The Art of Underwater Photography

3/1 The Aesthetics of Composition

I remember one evening in 1989 when I was heading out for a night dive during a photo shoot-out in Flores. Walking past a member of the jury, Gerald Soury from France, he beckoned my attention and told me "I hope you will make many good pictures." This stopped me to ponder... he did not use the word shoot or photograph but instead wished me to 'make' good pictures.

Through the years, I have practised following his wisdom. After learning how to play with the camera, there comes a point where you will be thinking about making a nice picture. I have learnt to appreciate photography as a form of fine art; our canvas is of course film and in digital, it is the sensor; the camera and lenses are the paint brushes and the medium in which we work is light.

Treat a photograph like a picture – it is a bunch of little details put together to make the whole. So plan the details, the focus, the statement, pick the big or small details to be part of your finished picture. We need to spend time working on understanding what it takes to make a photograph, not just the technical aspects but more importantly the artistic approach that must be included to get the end result. Approaching photography from this perspective, the science though essential is secondary, the artist in you is controlling the photographic process.

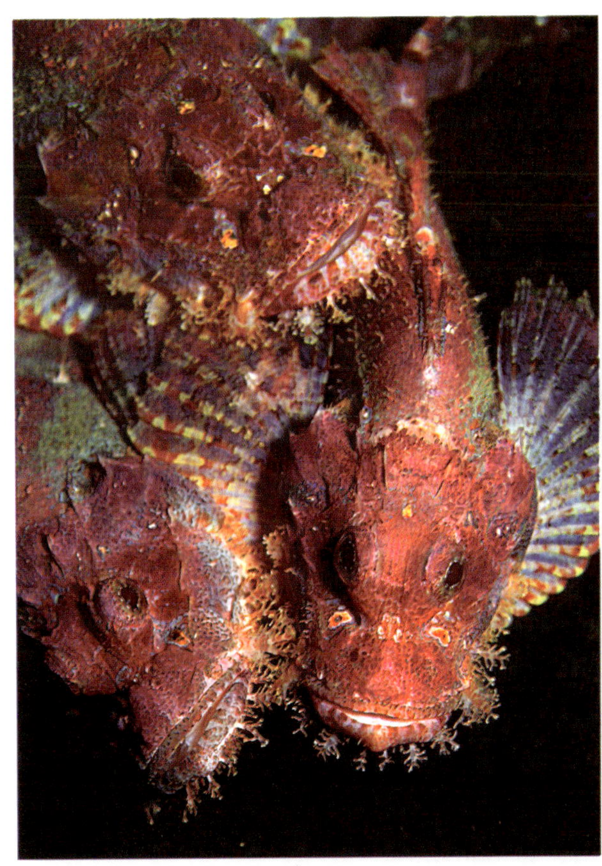

'Love on the Rock'
Scorpionfish courtship
Black Rock, Mergui
Nikon D1X, Seacam
housing, single Ikelite
S200, 1/2 power, f22,
1/60 sec, 60mm lens

Taking a picture is really simple – my two year old can do it just as well as you and I. Place the camera in a stable position and push the shutter shoot the picture – that is all it takes! But placing the camera in the right position is a very artistic kind of thing – it entails our perception, our point of view. Ask three photographers to shoot at the same subject and you may end up with three pictures of the same subject but with three different emphases, three different perspectives. Each picture reflects the photographer's point of view, and most often we will find one that is more appealing than the other two.

In composition we will learn about the lines, the horizon line, putting emphasis on the foreground, placed low you are placing importance on the upper part of the scene and we of course we need to pay attention to the intersections, where lines cross, where tones blend together and become one.

AWISM TO COMPOSITION

• *When the components of Art & Science are well integrated - they direct attention to dominant elements in the composition.*

• *The CENTRE or point of Interest should be the FOCUS of every thing in the picture. It can be a geometric centre or a dynamic centre.*

• *Only ONE IDEA should be the FOCUS in a single picture.*

• *This does not mean only one or few objects, rather the Composition should Support and EMPHASIZE the ONE Statement you wish to make.*

• *Irrelevant objects detract from the statement and should be eliminated.*

• *A 'lucky' shot is not taken by accident or by chance. It is well thought-out, well planned and well determined, well practised and when OPPORTUNITY arises - it just falls into place.*

• *Take time in composition, do not just take a photograph, make a picture instead.*

3/2 Types of Composition

Macro

Macro refers to pictures of relatively small subjects: nudibranchs, flatworms, small fishes and as well as parts of larger subjects (e.g. the eye of a parrotfish). These are easy to shoot as they move very slowly. They are great models for practising composition, lighting and exposure as adjustments can be made until the desired picture is achieved.

Shooting Macro with Prosumer cameras

1. Test the minimum focus range on land – install camera in housing. Use a small toy about 1" tall as a subject.

2. Set camera to macro mode.

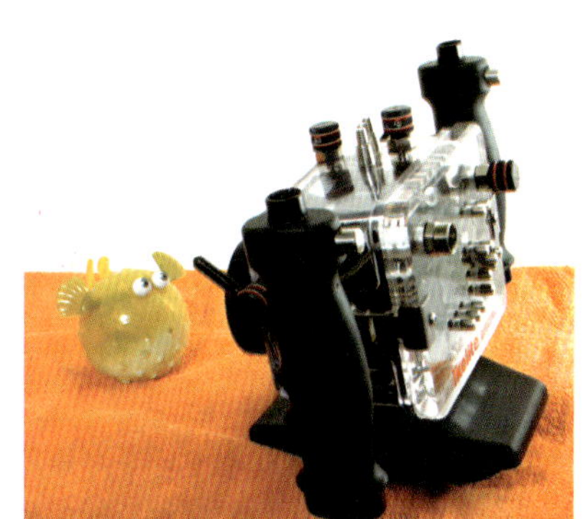

3. With focal length at the widest, move in as close as allowable while maintaining a sharp image in the LCD – once sharpness begins to reduce, pull back till image is sharp again – this is your minimum focusing distance.

4. Don't bother to zoom this will result in un-sharp images. For Extreme macro use add-on macro lenses e.g. Epoque DML-2 x 2.1, Inon UCL-165 and UCL-330 lenses.

Shooting Macro with a DSLR

1. The use of 1:1 macro lenses (Nikkor 60mm f2.8 Micro) is essential.

2. Start with the 60mm macro – remember with an entry level DSLR, you will gain a 1.6x multiplication of the focal length, making the 60mm an ideal lens.

3. Add-on closeup lens – this offers additional magnification but reduces the depth of field. 2T, 3T, 4T available.

4. Wet Lens – with some housings such as SEACAM, it is possible to purchase removable magnification lenses to use over the port system.

Wide-Angle Essentials

Wide-angle refers to pictures taken with lenses that can cover a large angle, greater than what can be seen by the human eye (46º picture angle / 50mm focal length - see chart). Portraits of large marine animals, seascapes, wrecks and even small subjects can be captured with wide-angle imagery.

Focal Length vs Area of Coverage

Focal Length (mm)	All Full-frame Fish eye	13 mm	14 mm	15 mm	18 mm	20 mm	24 mm	28 mm	35 mm	50 mm	55 mm	85 mm	100 mm	105 mm
Diagonal direction	180°	118°	114°	110°	100°	94°	84°	74°	62°	46°	43°	28° 30'	24°	23° 20'
Horizontal direction						83°	74°	64°	53°	39°	36° 10'	23° 50'	20°	19° 30'
Vertical direction						61°	53°	45°	37°	26°	24° 40'	16°	14°	13°

Wide angle pictures are windows to the sea and appeal even to non-divers, as they can easily relate to the scenery. Most prosumer cameras are limited to 28mm to 35mm as the widest focal length – as such the photographer would need to be about 8 metres away to shoot a 10 metre long subject. However, if one is using a 20mm lens, the distance is reduced to about 2 metres. **The advantage is obvious: the closer to the subject, the less water in front of the camera equals sharper image, more efficient use of artificial lighting.**

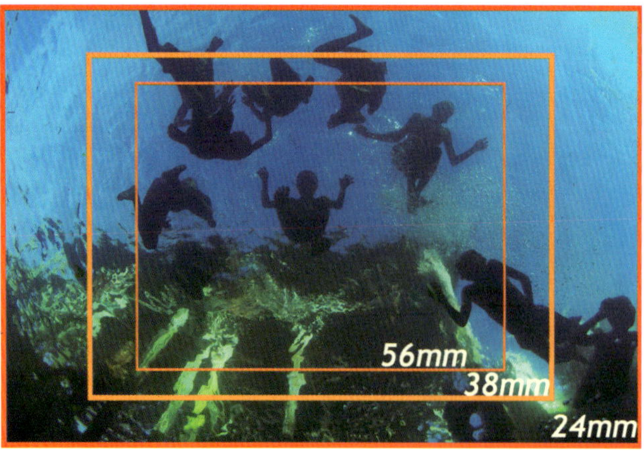

Effective Focal Length / coverage based on typical Prosumer/Consumer lenses.

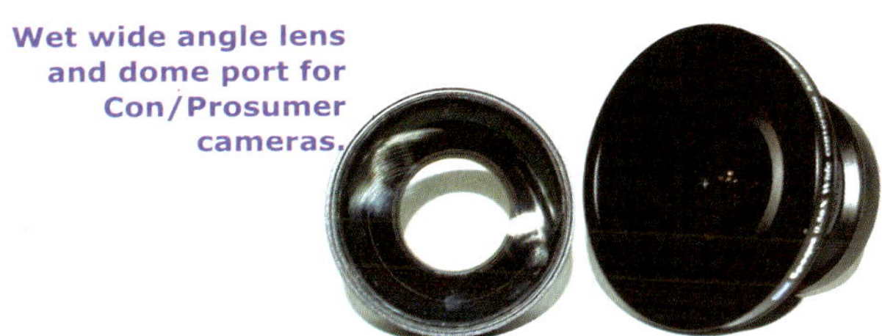

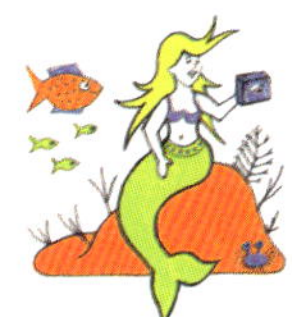

HINTS: to achieve small focal lengths for prosumer shooters.
1. Wet Add-on lenses – these are removable underwater with various equivalent focal lengths designated by magnification factor. Epoque DCL-20 lens (x 0.56), Inon UWL-105 (x0.53), the Aquatica (x0.63) lens. The smaller the magnification factor, the larger field of view.

2. Most add-on lenses result in vignetting (black corners in corner of image) – zoom in slightly to omit the black corners.

3. Dry add on lenses – available for most brands for topside use but for underwater, you will have to use housings that allows the use of changeable front ports: most Ikelite housings, some Olympus and the Aquatica A5000 housing for the Nikon Coolpix 5000.

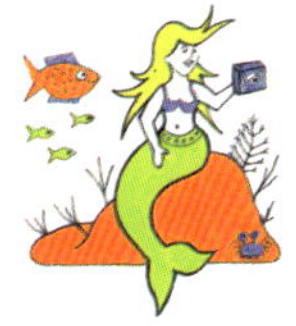

HINTS: for wide focal lengths - DSLR shooters
1. Generally all wide lenses can be used – 20mm, 18mm, 16mm, 14mm. Whereas you gain in macro, with an entry level DSLR, you will loose with the 1.6x multiplication of the focal length. A 16mm fisheye is equivalent to about 25mm. Fisheye is now possible with the Nikon 10.5mm.

2. The minimum starting range is therefore the 16mm. Nikon has a range of DSLR dedicated lenses – the 12-24mm zoom is recommended as the principal lenses for digital wide angle.

3. Use of a dome port is essential – ideally a combination of optical glass port, optically coated and specific optical centre to match the lenses you are using. Check with your housing manufacturer – if wide angle is your passion, insist on optical coating and optical glass ports.

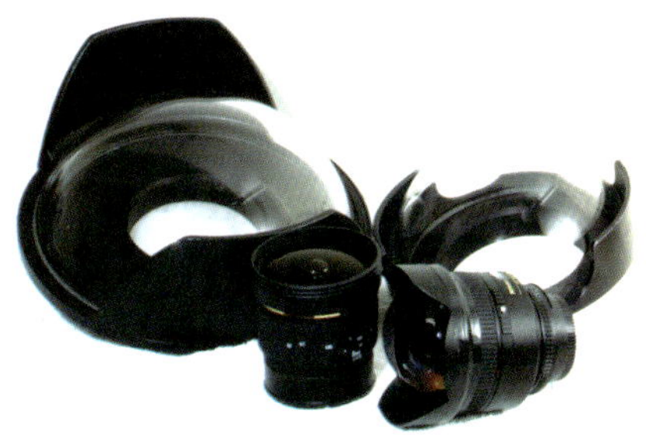

DSLR optical glass dome ports and lenses.

More Big Tips from the Photo Wizard

1. Subjects – choose subject of sizeable dimension or a sizeable scene. Generally one that includes vibrant colours, which will contrast with the blue water in the background. Situational wide-angle shots, those showing the interaction between two subjects (e.g. a fish at a cleaning station), or telling a story of life underwater (e.g. a school of fish on the reef), are those which are the most successful.

2. Select strobe with 110° angle of coverage.

3. Move in close to fill the frame – the desirable distance is less than 2 metres.

4. Get rid of the water – the closer the better.

5. Do not use zoom to photograph large subjects located far from the camera. Strobes will not likely be powerful enough to reach the subject and increased water column will result in a loss of definition.

6. Some add on lenses will trap air between the lens and the housing port during the descent. Remember to take out the lens and shake off any air bubbles that may have formed. These lenses are designed to have water to fill the space to work correctly.

'Seeing the Fan' Miri, Sarawak
This composition is an all time favourite for wide angle imagery. Just find the right fan, the right buddy, compose and shoot. Dual strobes are required for this image.

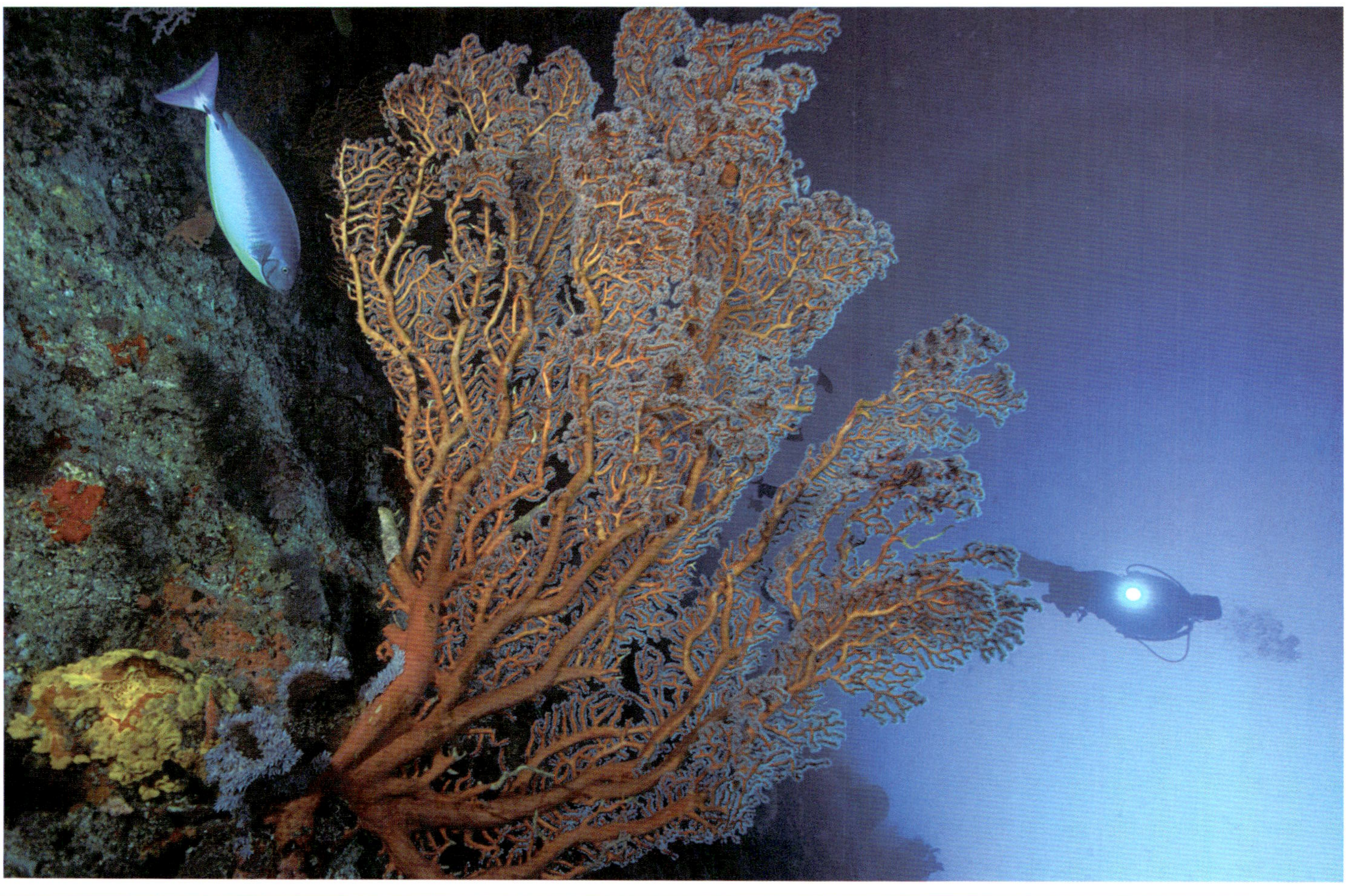

3/3 The Art of Composition

There could be many ways of composing a picture in an appealing manner. It all boils down to aesthetic preferences and story statements. It is often said that 'a picture is worth a thousand words', indeed but this can only be true if it has something to say! A picture must have a central theme or subject – without either it becomes a muddled image.

Composition 101 – identify a primary point of interest when composing a photograph. When you've determined the centre of focus, which is the most appealing to you, you can recompose to emphasize it. A great way to learn is to study advertising photography which in most instances focuses on the selling message of the composition.

For macro images the principal guideline is negate other elements in the picture that may compete with the main subject or statement: isolation is important. Background (negative space) must not overpower your subject but rather should emphasise the subject. The water column is often the best background for underwater images. It gives the sense of the aqueous environment and adds context to underwater imagery.

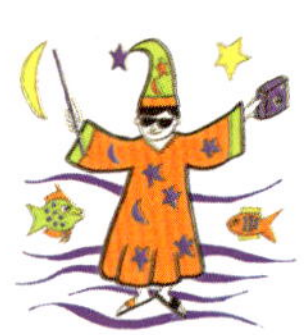

How to Compose 1, 2, 3, 4

1. Get below your subject and shoot up into open water.

2. One way of making your subject stand out is by use of different patterns or contrasting colours as a background.

3. The WOW factor is often dependant on colour. Pictures with loud colours such as red and yellow will grab the viewer's attention and make them stand out, so look for them.

4. Position, Position, Position – the position of your subject is critical and could make or ruin the image. Main subjects off centre will appear more pleasing to the eye. Bracket your positions.

Here are some broadly accepted rules of composition and shooting techniques which generally produce a different or better result. These should be taken as guidelines more than rules.

Orientation

Portrait or Landscape: It is all too common for beginners to confine themselves to landscape shots. Simply considering the portrait option doubles composition possibilities. Portrait shots can be adopted for a variety of subjects: fish portraits, walls, critters, etc. Portraits often give a different perspective that is much more interesting composition-wise. Portraits are also money shots – they are shots for front covers of magazines and yield between $200 to $2000. To have this flexibility, you should make your system adapted to quick changes between landscape and portrait shots. (see pic) Strobe arm configuration should allow you to re-position your strobes quickly, and to place them adequately for both landscape and portrait shots.

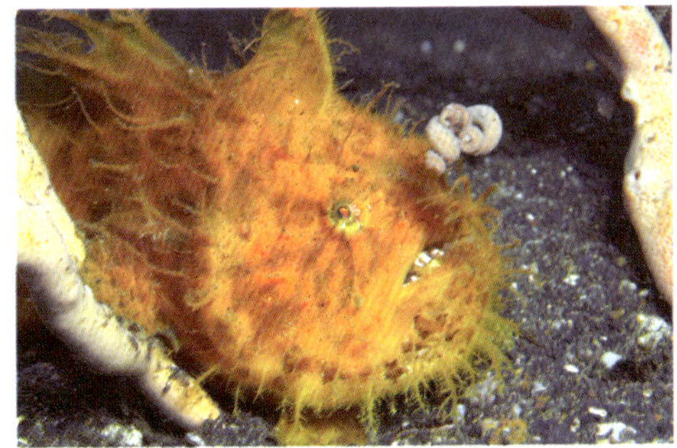

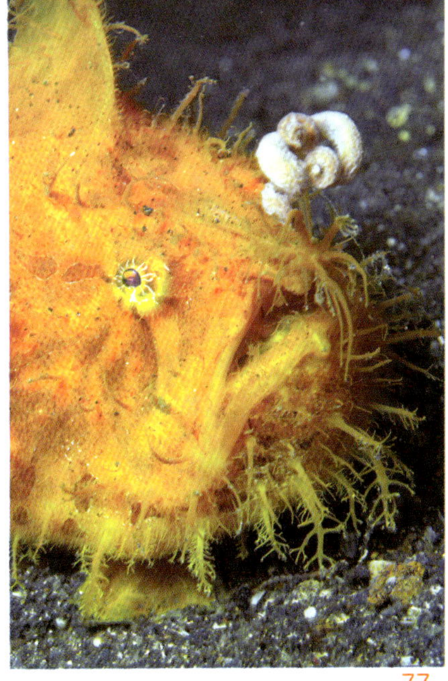

Here are 2 shots of a Hairy frogfish – one ended up as a front cover of Asian Geographic magazine – it pays to bracket orientation.

The Rule of Thirds

We attribute the rule of thirds to the Greek artists and scientists alike that have quantified what makes good design or composition. The concept of the "golden rule" has come to influence classical drawing and sculpture. Divide your composition into thirds both vertically and horizontally; dominant subject should usually fall onto one of the four interest areas or points you have created.

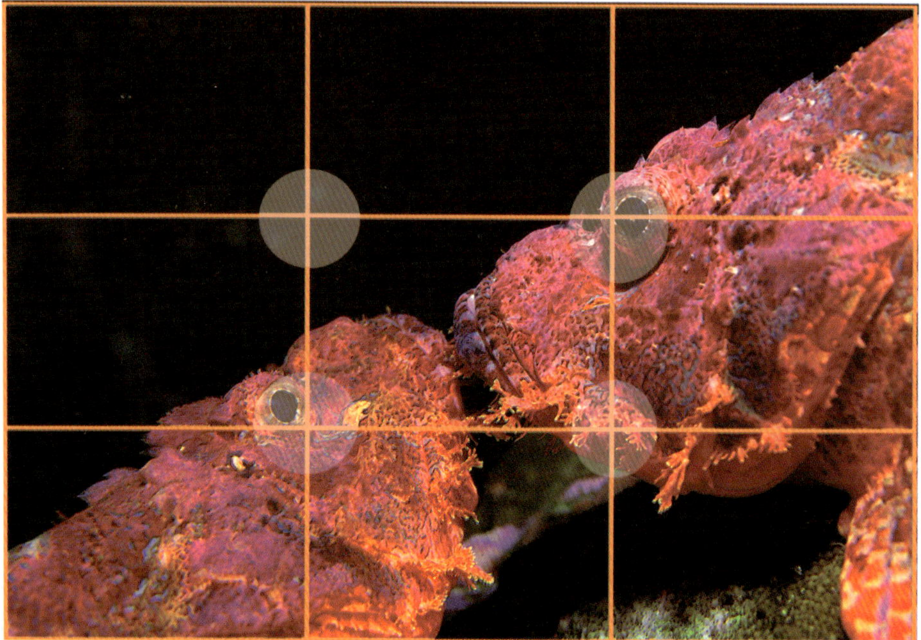

This is an absolute use of the Rule of Third where two focal points are used to direct you to the geometric centre of the picture.

The ideal placing of subject at one of these cross points will create an image that is more powerful and able to keep the interest of the viewer. It gives a feeling of flow, direction and harmony, and keeps the subject from being dull. Too often, placing the subject in the centre of the image makes the picture look posed. The guide is for an asymmetrical composition where the subject is not centred or if it is centred, the eye of the subject should be at one of the cross points. Again, this is a very general rule. You don't have to target the exact intersection point, but simply these general areas. Also, although this "rule" offers interesting compositions in most cases, there are shots where it may not be applicable and for which another type of composition may yield more pleasing results.

Principles of Foreground and Negative Space

1. An obviously un-sharp foreground is distracting – such images are almost always thrown out during judging at photo competitions.

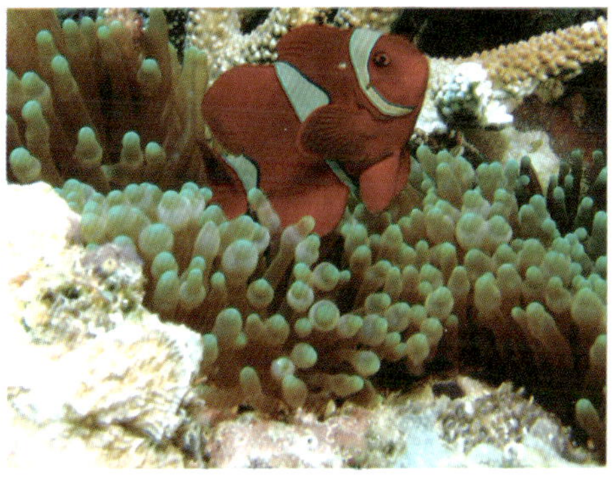

2. Negative space is any object or element within a photographic frame that is not the subject – essentially the area of the picture surrounding the subject. Skilled fine art artists and photographers know that the treatment of negative space is often the difference between an ordinary picture and a masterpiece.

3. While the pose of the subject and the technical aspects are important factors, in some cases the vital factor that makes a particular picture more compelling is not that the fish or squid is more striking than all the rest, but that the other elements in the frame make the image different and more special.

4. Clever use of negative space creates a textural contrast and accentuates interest on the subject.

5. Composing a subject against a background of a completely different colour can create contrast – it helps bring out and emphasize the dominant element. By improving contrast, it enhances aesthetic appeal.

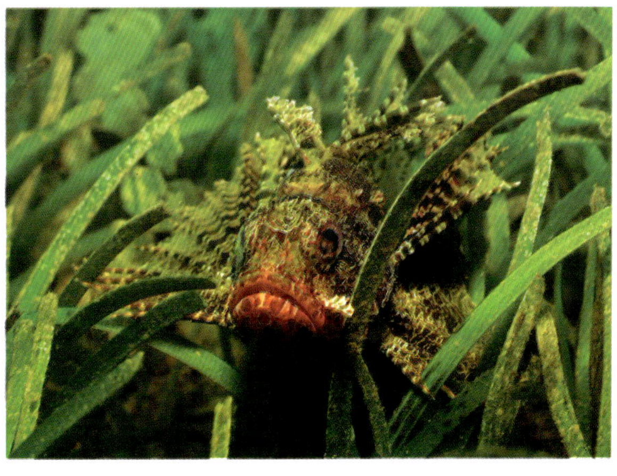

It helps define the subject better by making it stand out, and the use of contrasting colours is pleasing to the eye.

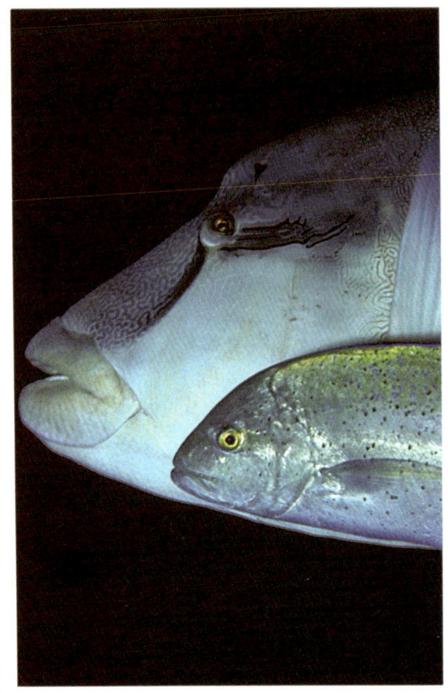

This Napoleon wrasse needs some nose room to breathe.

Take time in composition - take in the whole subject.

Breathing Space - Noseroom and Headroom

Especially when working with fish and mammals, your subject needs to breath – you must give them enough headroom and noseroom: if the subject is too large in the frame, to the point of being very close to the edges, the subject appears constrained, boxed up, and the resulting image is not very appealing to the eye. However too much space may make the subject appear too small – ideally, your subject should occupy at least 25% of the frame in order to be adequately conspicuous as the main subject.

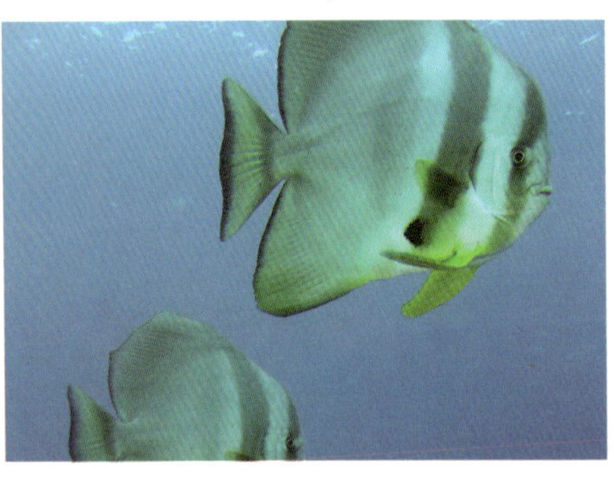

Completeness of Subject

Before you actually press the shutter release, have a last look at the LCD or viewfinder, and make sure that your subject is complete. This doesn't necessarily mean that the whole fish is in the frame, but if you're doing a fish portrait, its head should be completely in. One very common example of incompleteness is the tail of a fish being chopped off at the edge of a shot. This tends to be damaging to the shot, as the viewer expects to see the subject in its completeness. Similarly, it is important to ensure that no alien elements have crept their way into the picture. This tends to have a very distracting effect, and can potentially destroy an otherwise perfect picture. A very common example is the hand or fin of a dive buddy tucked in the corner of a picture.

Directional Lines

Use of real or imaginary lines in composition leads the eye into the dominant element. These lines can be vertical, horizontal, diagonal or even curving across the frame. Linear elements such as sea whips, trumpet fish or a sea fan placed diagonally are generally perceived as more dynamic than horizontal lines.

By using diagonal lines instead, you can achieve much richer compositions. These add dimension and dynamism to the picture by leading the viewer from one area to the other, and emphasizing the special relationship between the different elements in the picture.

This results in shots which are generally pleasing. Once again, this rule is just a general guideline and may not be applicable to all situations (e.g. shooting under a pier, with vertical pillars).

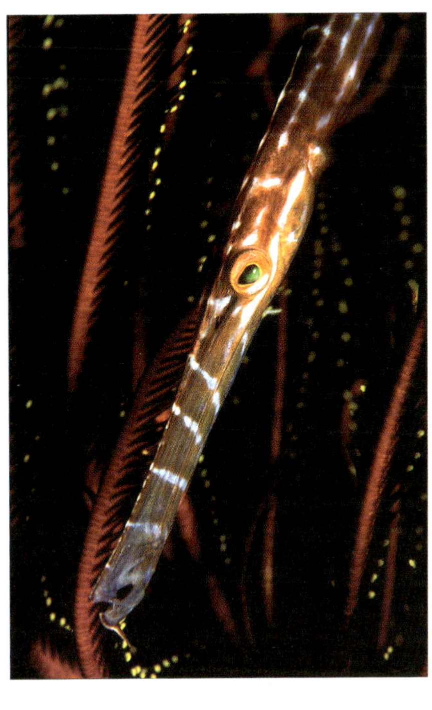

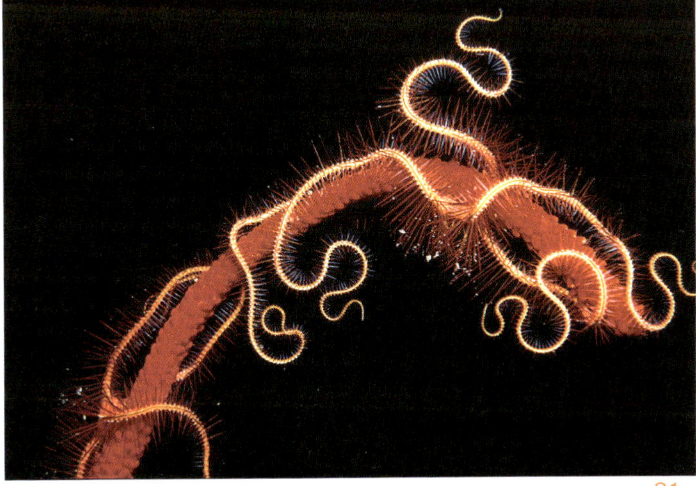

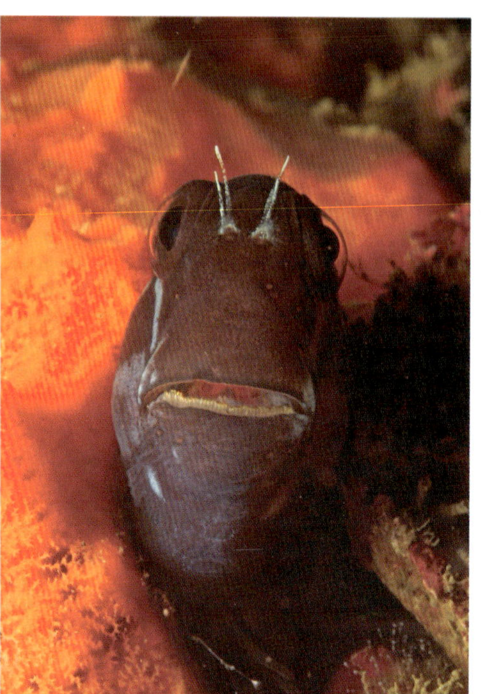

One Eye, Two eyes

Eyes are essential in portraits – they must be sharp and there must be eye contact; they will be looking at the viewer or pointing towards a subject in the frame. Eye contact pictures are dramatic; eyes of shrimp, fish, mantis shrimp eyes on stalks give great impact to a portrait.

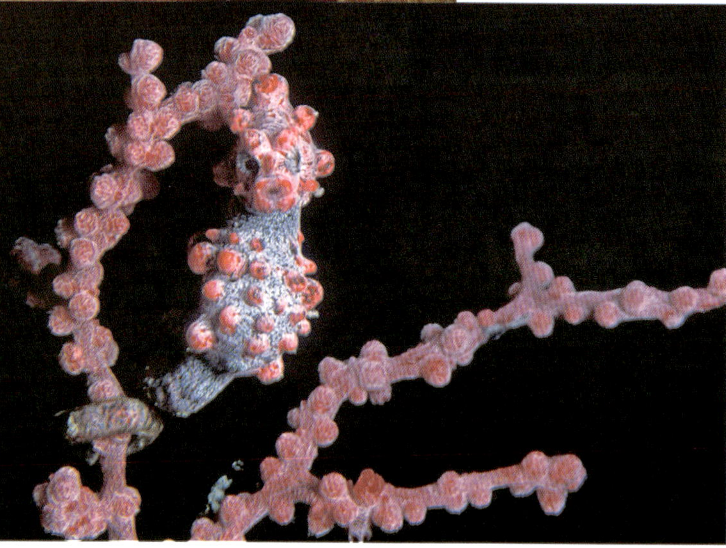

The bulbous eyes of the blenny and moray eel add a sense of menace to a face. Now the challenge, two eyes is better than one – a picture of a blenny or seahorse with two eyes in frame and in focus is more inspiring than one. ***Get in close - establish eye contact, establish an eye to eye conversation.***

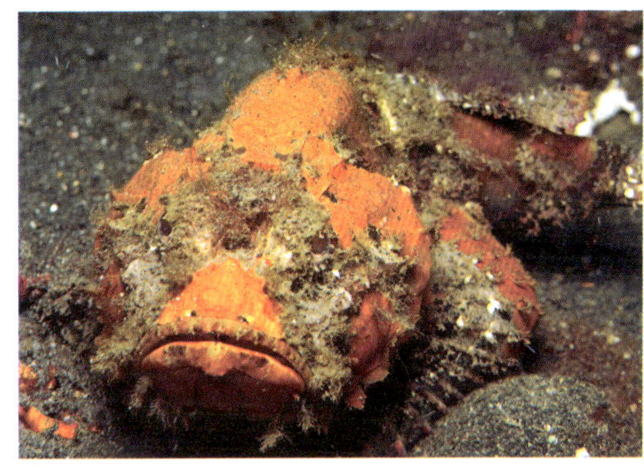

Directional Rules

1. The direction of the subject is vital in a picture – I learnt this from the film school – Bad guys come from the right – it contradicts our thoughts. Good guys come from the left – it is natural to us – it is the way we read.

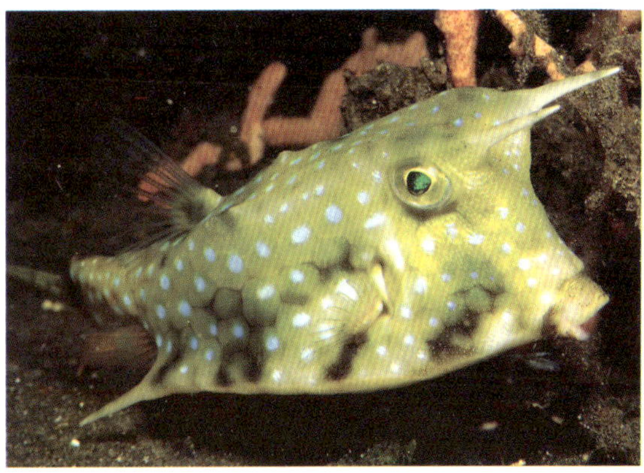

2. Fish tails and divers fins are poor subjects. A fish or diver coming into the scene leads the viewer into the picture. For real drama, a fish swimming towards the lens will give wow impact.

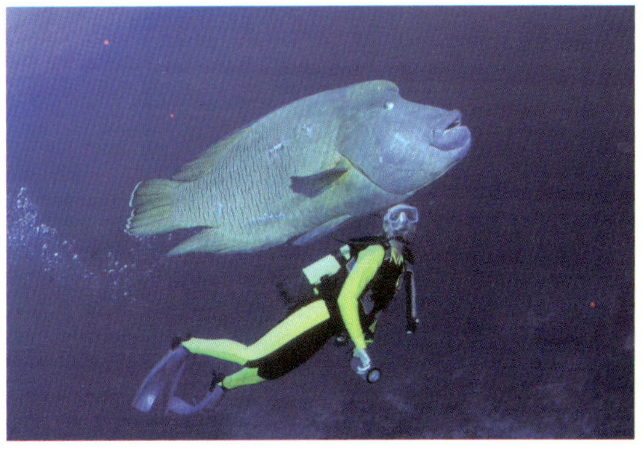

3. Direction of movement: fish, turtles, divers are capable of movement - leave space in front of the subject so it appears to be moving into, rather than out of, the photograph.

Third Element - Divers

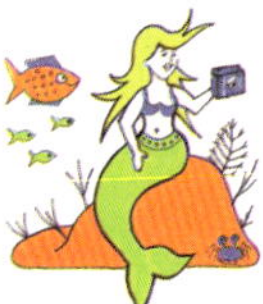

HINTS: Because size, scale and distance is difficult to comprehend in underwater images, an interesting technique to improve the appeal of underwater imagery is by adding a diver to the picture.

1. A diver at work, exploring or interacting with marine animals provides strong subject matter – a diver taking photographs can prove interesting, especially if their subject is also in the image. Use a torch to highlight the secondary subject suggesting exploration and encounter.

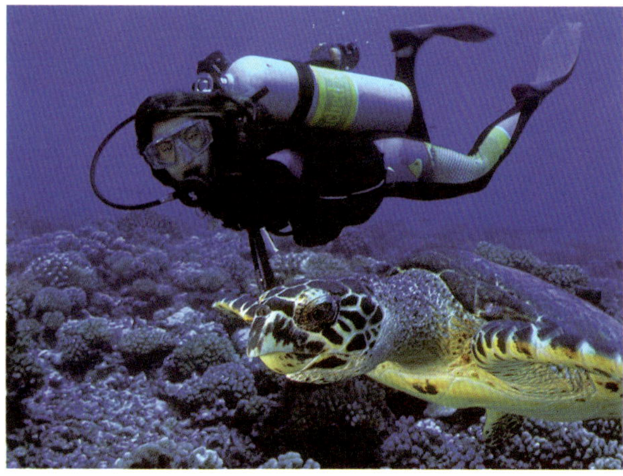

2. Poses should be avoided; your model should look comfortable. It is often best if they don't look directly at the camera, but at some other subject within the frame. This creates a dynamic that leads the viewers' eyes from the diver, to that other subject. Remember to check their feet, legs together looks better than legs and fins spread wide.

3. Ensure your model is not seen to be holding onto anything fragile, especially coral. This is unacceptable in good underwater imagery.

4. Another key element is communication. The model must be briefed on the shot you want to achieve and what you expect from them. Also, it is a good idea to have your own set of hand signals for underwater communication. These could include signals for "Go back!", "Start again!", "Look there!", "Turn your body!".

5. Action – have your model on the move or doing something. Altogether, they help make the image even better.

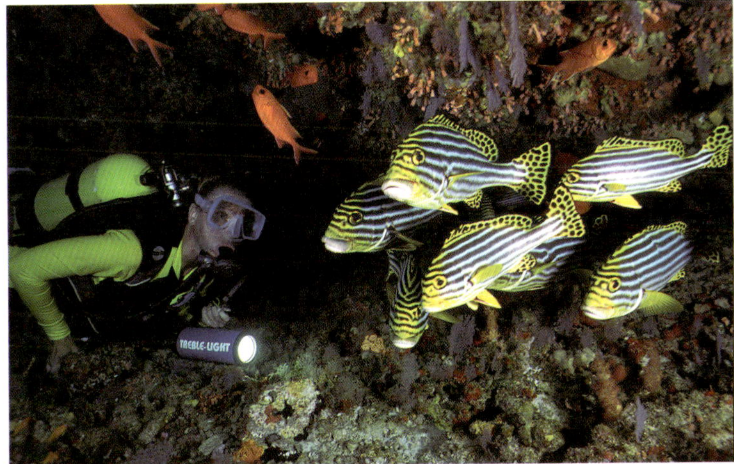

6. The diver's eyes always provide a point of interest; they should convey amazement, fear or curiosity. They should act as pointers to the main subject, e.g. a diver looking at a group of sweetlips. For this to work, your model should wear a mask that offers a clear view of their face, as being able to see their eyes emphasises the dynamics of the composition.

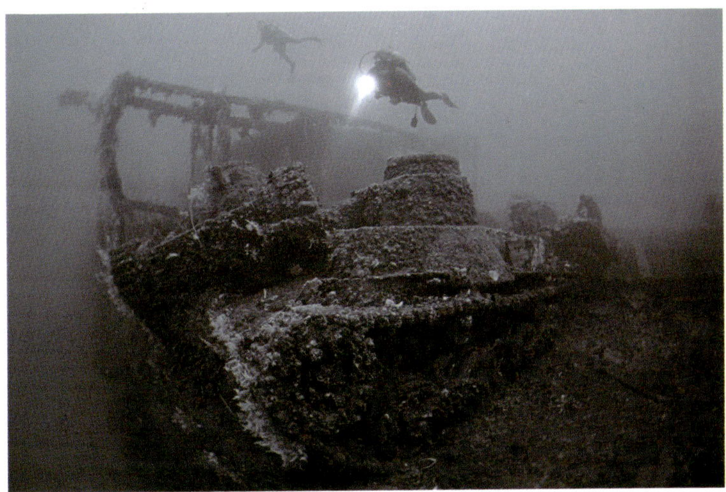

7. Wrecks – a diver gives an indication of the size of the wreck. Unless there is lush marine growth, wrecks are dull in colour – use your buddy to add colour wearing brightly coloured diving equipment Or shoot in black and white – wrecks are perfect for black and white photography.

Module Four
The Digital Darkroom

4/1 Picture Management

Just like in film photography, the digital photographic process continues after a trip. Previously, the continuation required processing film, reviewing and culling images, cataloguing and storing them for various uses. It is essential that you follow the same discipline. However, instead of good old fashioned film, you will be working with the digital medium.

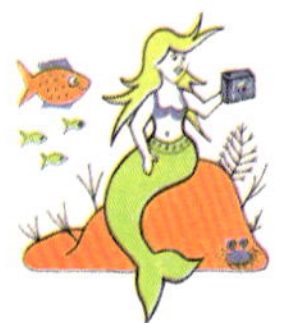

Processing and Managing Pictures

Set up a dedicated desktop PC or Mac as your digital workstation. Essentially the faster the CPU, the better. It is also best to have an extra hard drive dedicated to storing images. Again, get the biggest capacity that your budget allows. USB2 and Firewire 1394 interface is essential for speedy download. A CRT monitor is the industry standard and always better than LCD screen.

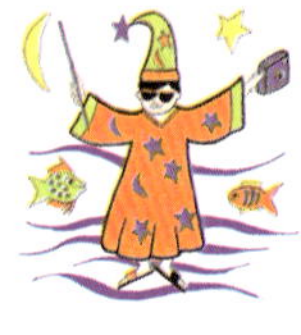

How to Manage Digital Stock?

1. In the assigned hard drive, create a new folder, naming it after the location you have just been to (e.g. LEMBEH_2004).

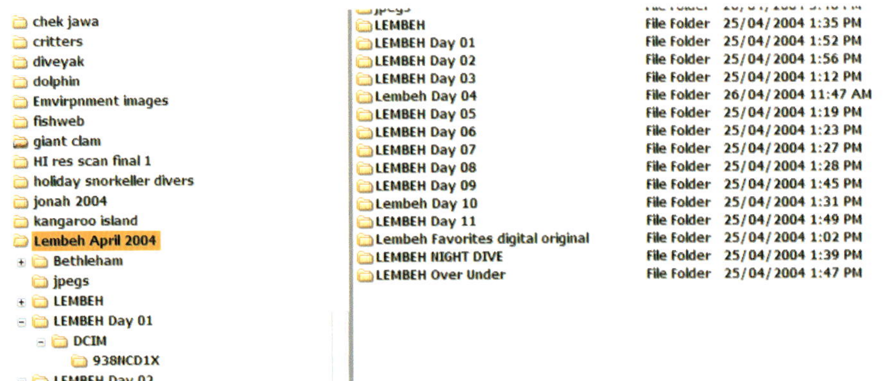

2. Create subfolders and name according to the day and sites of your trip.

3. Transfer images from your portable storage device (see module one) or storage media to respective folders. Rename all the images using the trip location as prefix (e.g. 'MDO_xx.jpg', where 'xx' is a running number). Renaming using Windows XP is an easy process. Alternatively, another convenient tool is Batch Rename (www.stintercorp.com), which allows you to rename a whole group of files at once.

4. Create a new subfolder in Lembeh_2004 and name it Favourites or Lembeh Favorites digital originals.

5. Review images with a photo viewing software e.g. Olympus CamediaMaster, NIKONVIEW, or a third party software such as ACDSee or Foto Station. For DSLR shooters, you may wish to use Bibble (www.bibblelabs.com). This software is one of the swiftest and most accurate programmes for processing RAW files.

6. Using thumbnail view, review all the pictures one by one, and delete those that are not worth keeping (totally blue, incomplete or blurred subject, etc.). Select those that you feel are special or have good potential, and save them as TIFF files (uncompressed) in the Favourites folder.

How to Manage Digital Stock? (cont'd)...

7. Process your favourite pictures using a photo editing software. Photoshop is the industry standard. (see the 'How to Process' section). Save and close after each image.

8. Back up all the folders from the trip onto CDs, DVDs or another hard drive. Hard drives are fragile devices, and can therefore fail. It is better to pre-empt any potential problem.

Critical Note:

JPEG images undergo 'lossy' compression during use; lossy because some of the image information is discarded during the saving process. Regardless of the choice of 'Quality' setting, some information will still be lost. To make matters worse, every time you open and close a jpeg image information will be lost, regardless of whether you have made any changes to the image or not.

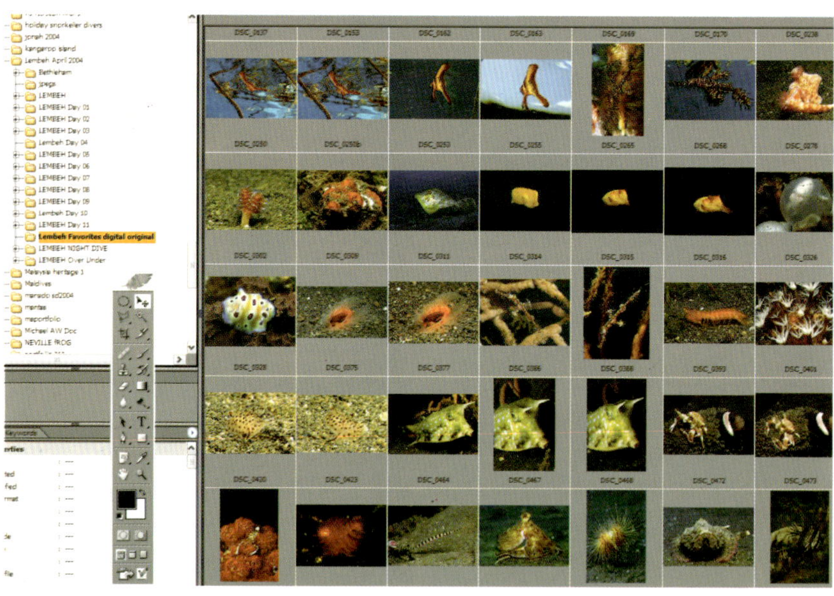

Selected images are organised into a Favorites folder post post editing. In this instance the original raw (NEF) file name is preserved as reference for later use.

The Digital Darkroom

A conventional darkroom is comprised of an enlarger, trays of harmful chemicals, timer, plastic colour filters, masking films and an array of lenses to reproduce or enhance raw images. The digital equivalent is a desktop computer loaded with a fast CPU, lots of RAM and hard disk storage space, and an image editing software such as Adobe Photoshop Elements, JASC Paintshop Pro, ULead PhotoImpact or Adobe Photoshop. The latter has become the industry standard in photo editing.

Like judicious dodging/burning, colour filters and lenses, and variable contrast printing papers were used to produce photos of Ernest Brooks II, Brett Weston and Ansel Adams, editing programs essentially do the same, but in a cleaner and more comfortable environment. However, a lot has been said about Photoshop being the cheating process to good pictures. Unless one is referring to dropping in subjects which are not in the picture in the first place (this is also done in conventional darkrooms for the advertising trade), the digital enhancement process is very similar to techniques used by the great masters of photography.

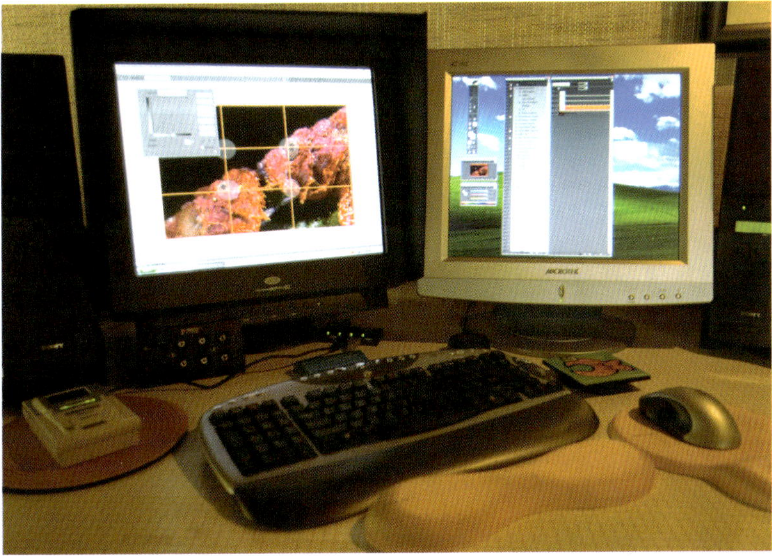

Just like a film darkroom, it is best to have an editing suite in a dark environment – add a hood to the main monitor – this helps you to see pictures in better colour rendition. If budget allows, use a second monitor for tool palettes and the main monitor to see images in the biggest possible size.

Ethics in Digital Manipulation – Acceptable Standards

There is no way a photograph or painted canvas can be a true reproduction of reality. The final picture in both media is an interpretation by the image maker, modified and distorted by paints, canvas or film, sensors, lenses and exposure values.

Assuming setting the same exposure, to shoot the same scene, using the same camera using Fuji Velvia and Kodak VS 100 ISO films, the result will be two pictures with differing hue, colour rendition, contrast and brightness. Likewise in digital photography, images captured by an Olympus 5 megapixel camera will differ from one captured by a Nikon 5 megapixel camera.

While standards in manipulation vary greatly between the 'glamour' and the traditional photographic magazines, the 'acceptable' standard among ethical photographers is to limit the use of software-based editing functions to those equivalents in the traditional film darkroom. Ironically for publishing purposes, film images must also be digitally scanned and enhanced for the printing process. The general guideline thus allowed for manipulation is that the enhanced image should be as close as possible to the actual scene. An average photograph is still an average photograph but an easier enhancement process is possible with a digital darkroom. By prudent use of editing tools, we can certainly make a very good picture great, or at least turn a good picture into a very good picture. It may help a bad picture become more viewable but it still remains a bad picture.

Critical Note:

Before you start any enhancement process make sure that your images are recorded in raw or converted to tiff format. Avoid any in-camera enhancement process including sharpening and remember JPEG files are compressed and they would have already been degraded by the camera.

CALIBRATING MONITORS – for printed pictures to look as they display on the screen, it is essential to calibrate your monitor. This will ensure that the colours you get on the paper are as close as possible to those you see on the screen.

Quick options: Praxisoft's WiziWYG (freeware), QuickGamma (freeware) and Adobe Gamma (bundled with Photoshop). Follow the calibration instructions to produce a working profile. For reliability, dedicated hardware such as the Colorvision Spyder with PhotoCal or OptiCal is recommended.

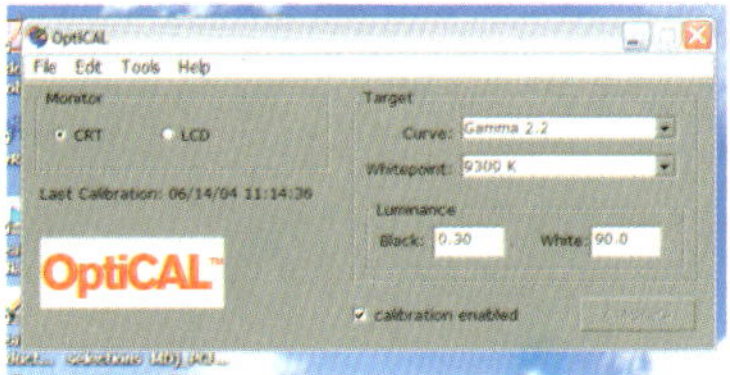

If you require accurate colour reproduction, dedicated hardware and software must be used to reliably calibrate your monitor profile. Do this at least once a month.

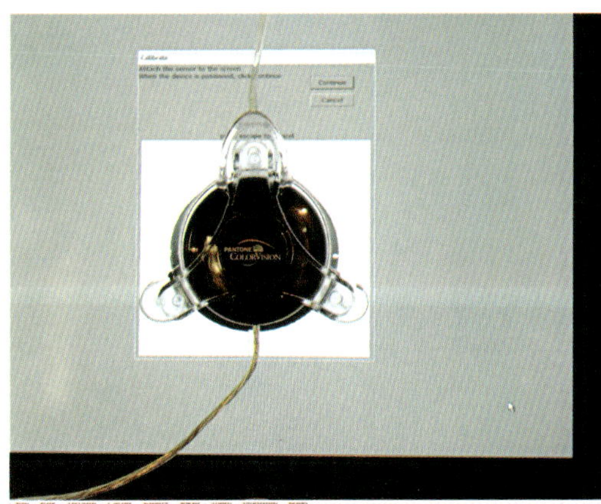

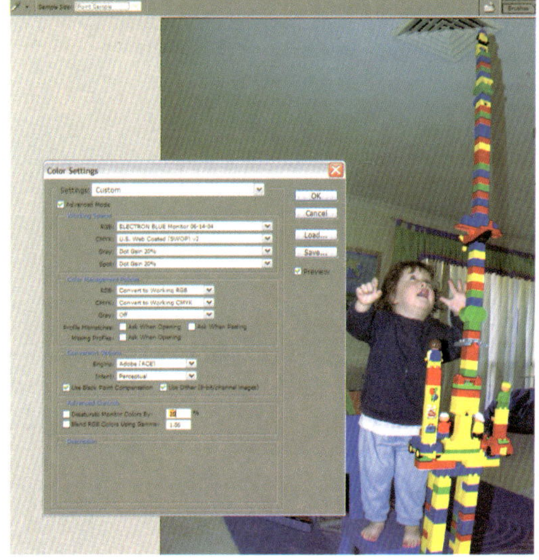

It is important also to set working space in your editing software to use the calibrated profile. In Photoshop – EDIT>Color Settings > RGB: select profile.

4/2 How to process digital images with Photoshop

CROPPING AND ROTATING PICTURES

1. If the image is shot in vertical/portrait orientation, rotate right side up by: Image > Rotate Canvas > 90º CW or 90º CCW

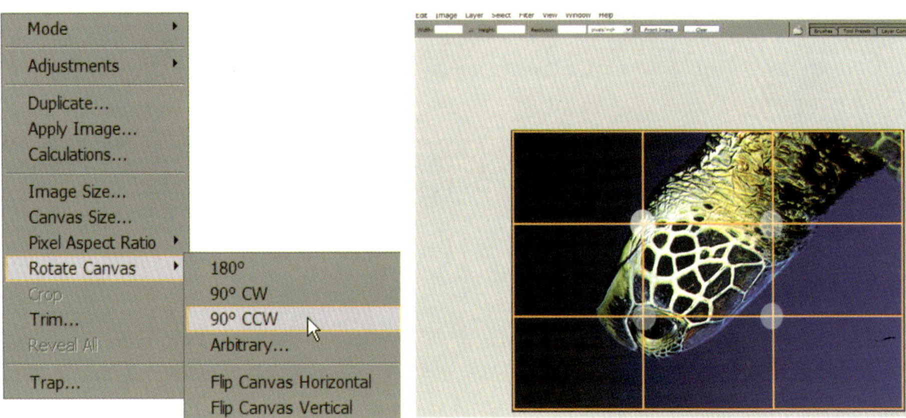

2. Cropping (e.g. to remove unwanted bits, blurred foregrounds or simply to improve balance): in the tool box > click on Crop tool> drag to create a box highlighting the area that you want to keep, > double-click or press 'Enter'.

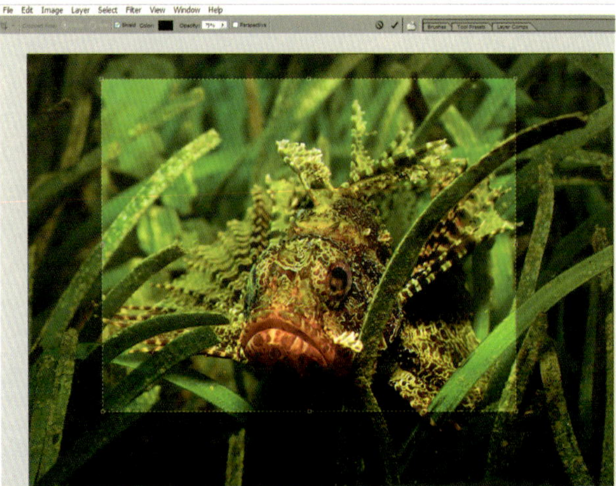

3. Sometimes Arbitrary rotation is required to better balance an image (especially if you have the horizon in the picture): Image > Rotate Canvas > Arbitrary (insert angle clockwise or anti clockwise).

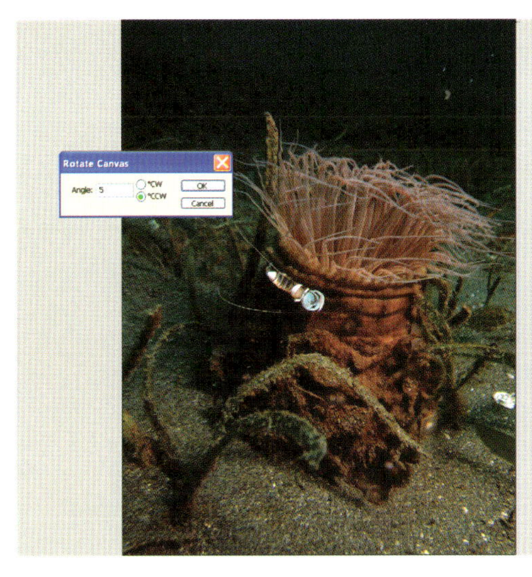

OR

activate the 'Crop' function, drag to create a box highlighting the area that you want to keep > place mouse just outside one of the corners >click and drag the mouse to rotate the selected area > place mouse back into the selected area > double click or press 'Enter'.

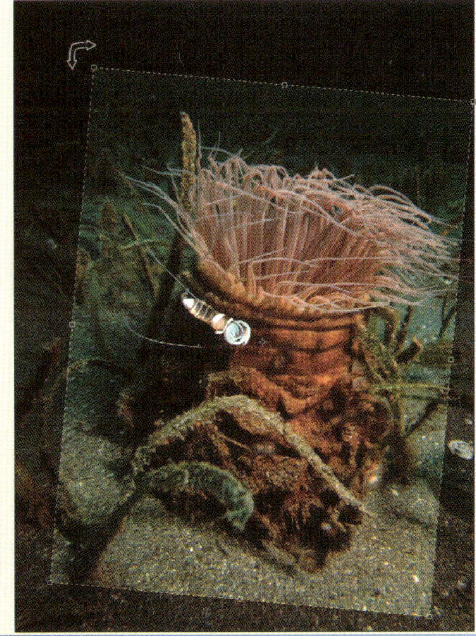

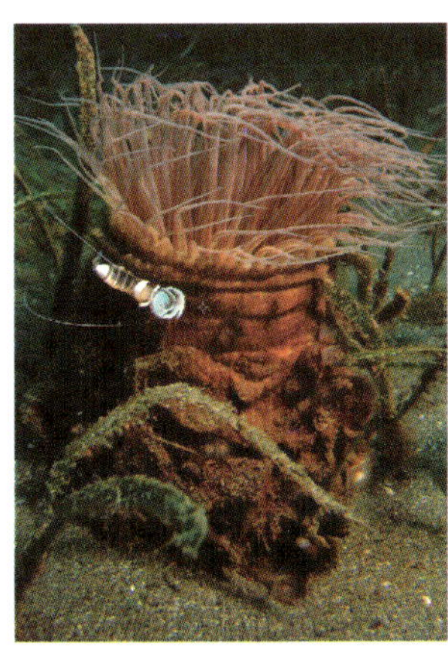

CORRECTING EXPOSURE AND COLOUR - QUICK FIX

Light decreases and colours are eliminated as we go deeper. 'Warm' colours are the first to disappear underwater. An easy way to enhance exposure and colours is to use of the 'Auto-Color', 'Auto Contrast' and 'Auto-Levels' tools.

Image > Adjustments > 'Auto-Color' or 'Auto Contrast' or 'Auto-Levels'

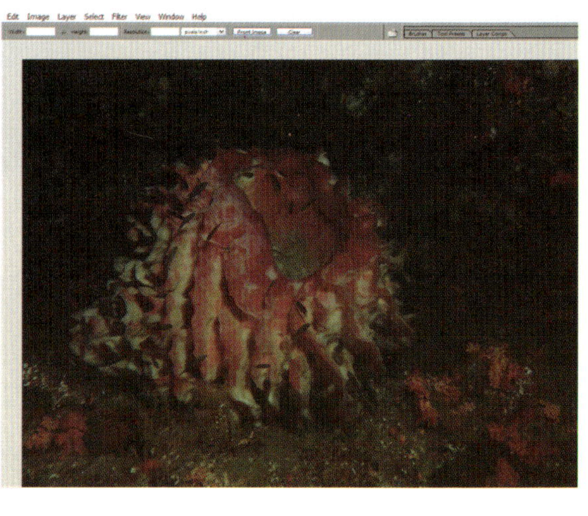

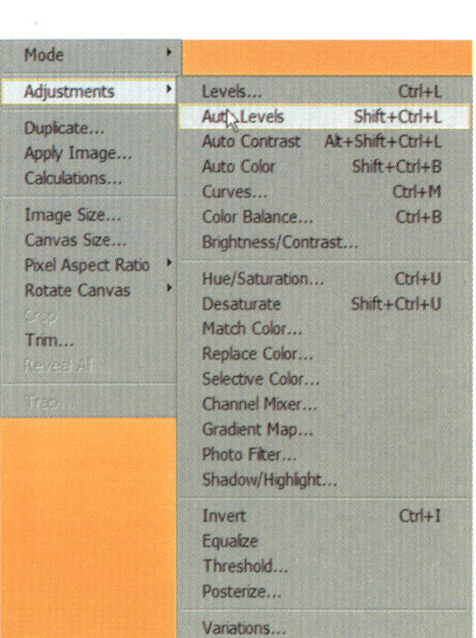

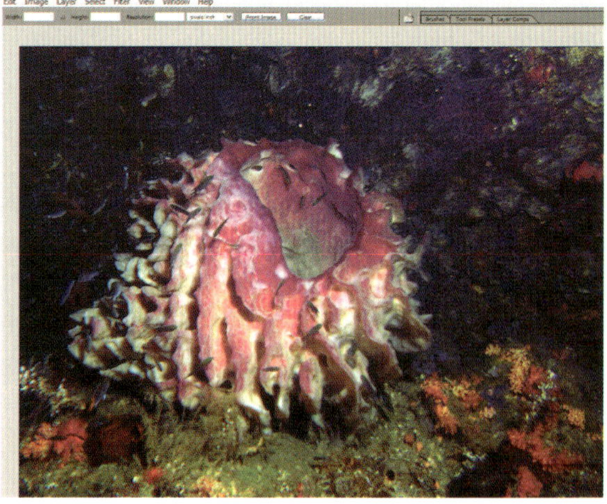

In some cases, these tools will give pretty good results, increasing the contrast, boosting brightness and re-gaining some of the lost colours. However, these are crude tools and can result in 'over-correction', especially with blue water pictures making the images a shocking pink and black.

Advanced Fixes

Advanced fixes consist of using the 'Levels' or 'Curves' tools. These allow the correction of all colours simultaneously, thereby correcting the contrast and brightness, or individual colour channels and so balancing colours in the picture (e.g. strengthen the red component). Colour channels represent the 'Red', 'Green' and 'Blue' components which are mixed together to form the 'full colour' picture displayed on your computer.

Understanding the HISTOGRAM

The histogram of the image will be displayed when you call up the Levels dialogue box. It represents the distribution of various colours or shades of pixels according to their total count in the picture. The histogram illustrates the distribution of light values in the image with a range of typically 256 values, from darkest to lightest, with the vertical axis showing the amount.

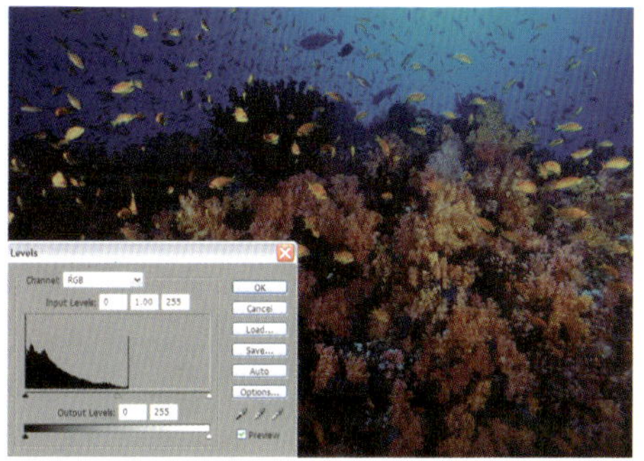

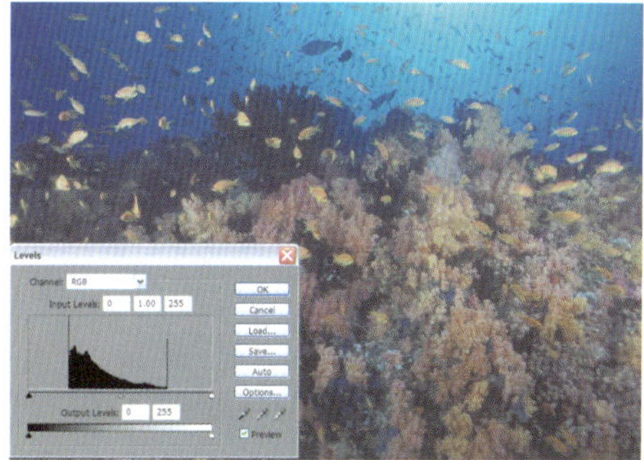

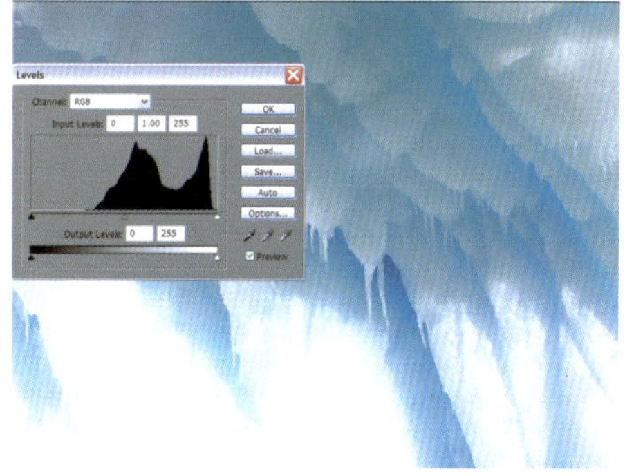

1. If the whole histogram is shifted towards the left, with almost nothing left on the right hand side, the picture is generally underexposed.

2. If the histogram is concentrated around the centre, with almost nothing on the left and right sides, the picture lacks contrast (the image lacks black and white, mostly 'average' grey tones).

3. If a peak is present on the extreme right of the histogram, this indicates there are numerous white pixels, which means that part of the image is overexposed.

'Adjustment Layers' in Photoshop

A layer in Photoshop is like a piece of clear film overlaying an image. This layer can contain another image or text and can be resized or repositioned separately from your main picture. A layer can be switched on or off and merged with the main picture or layers above and beneath it. To process digital images with Photoshop, the best option is to use an 'Adjustment Layer' for each enhancement. This is done by clicking on Layer > New Adjustment Layer to adjust for brightness, contrast and colour balance.

The main problem of digital image processing is that every time you make a change to a digital picture you will slightly degrade it. There's no way to change the contrast and then later change it again without image degradation. This is the main reason for using Adjustment Layers to preserve the quality of the main image. Any changes made to the image using an Adjustment Layer are not done to the image itself, but to an overlay which can be switched on and off, or removed at any time.

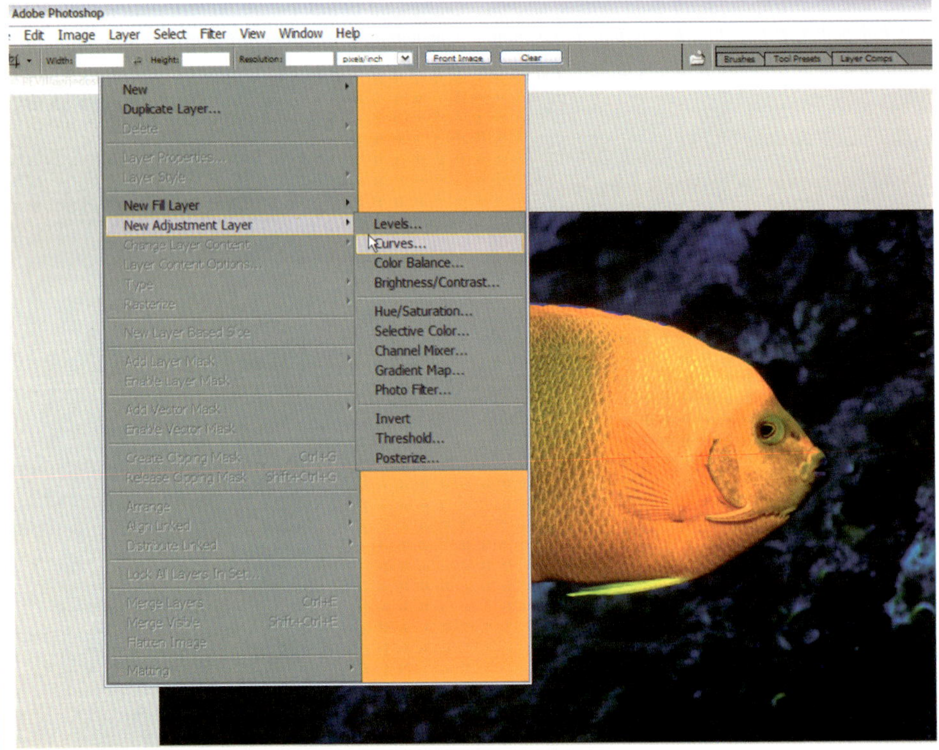

How to process Brightness / Contrast and Colour Adjustments

Level adjustment: For photographers, this is the most useful tool in Photoshop. It allows altering brightness, contrast and colour balance in one single step.

1. Click Layer > New Adjustment Layer > Levels.

2. A 'New Layer' window named 'Levels 1' will appear – click OK.

3. A 'Levels' window appears.

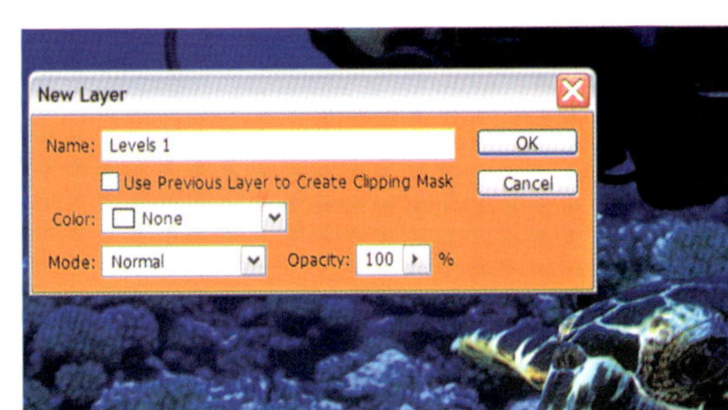

4. The three essential tools are the left, right and centre Input Levels triangular sliders.

• Use the black one on the left to make the image darker.

• Use the white one on the right to make it lighter.

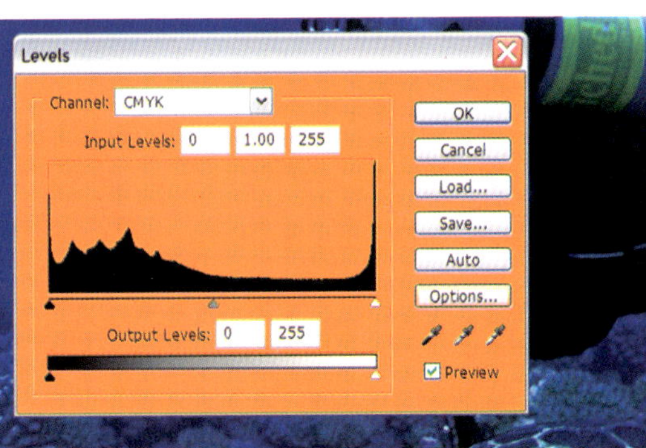

• Move both black and white sliders inwards to increase contrast.

• Use the grey centre slider to make changes to the overall brightness of the image.

• The Output Levels sliders at the bottom of the window allows you to decrease contrast and brightness.

5. Once you've adjusted the sliders to achieve a pleasing tonality – you can click on the 'Preview' check box to see the before and after enhancement of the image.

6. On the Channel selector box on the top which now indicates RGB, click on the drop down selection box to access the Red, Blue and Green channels independently. By working with each of these channels you can now change the colour balance of the image, the dynamic range of each channel and the image's overall colour tonality.

7. Once you've adjusted one or at most two of the colour channels, go back and adjust the RGB channel to make any final overall corrections to the image's brightness and contrast. Click OK to close the window and accept the changes.

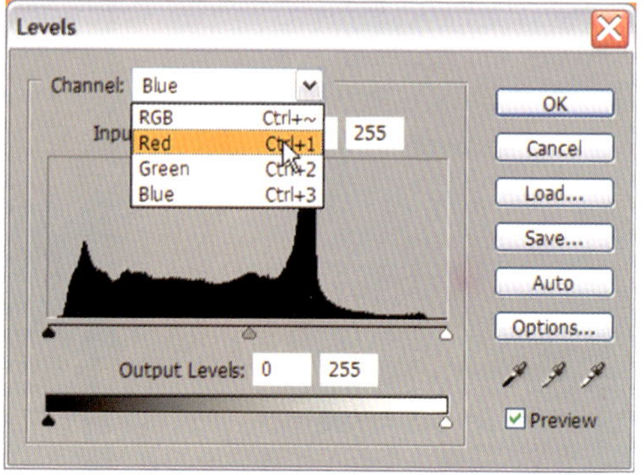

8. You may choose to look at the Show Layers / Window. You will see that a new layer has been created called 'Levels 1'. This layer contains the changes that you just made. You can turn the layer off at any time by clicking the eye-icon located next to it thus turning off the changes.

9. Further changes can be made by double clicking on the histogram in the 'Levels' layer in the palette selector to recall the Levels tool.

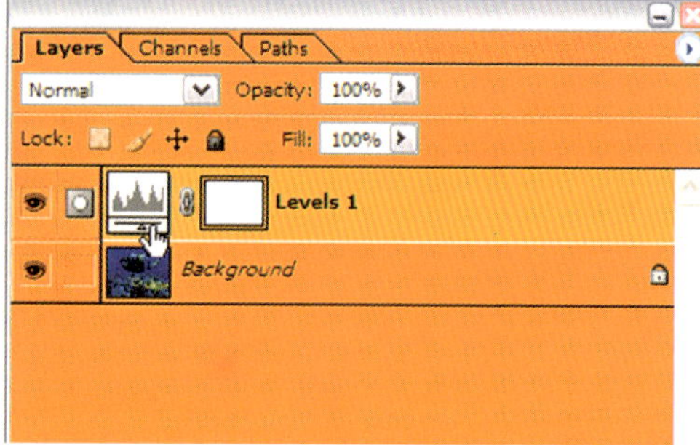

10. With the Levels Histogram window displayed again, further changes with the left, right and centre input level triangular sliders.

11. You can also create another new Levels layer and make additional changes to it. This is useful when you want to see what further changes will do without disrupting what you have previously done.

Advanced Hint

1. Look out for the small window named Opacity on the top right hand corner of the Layers palette.

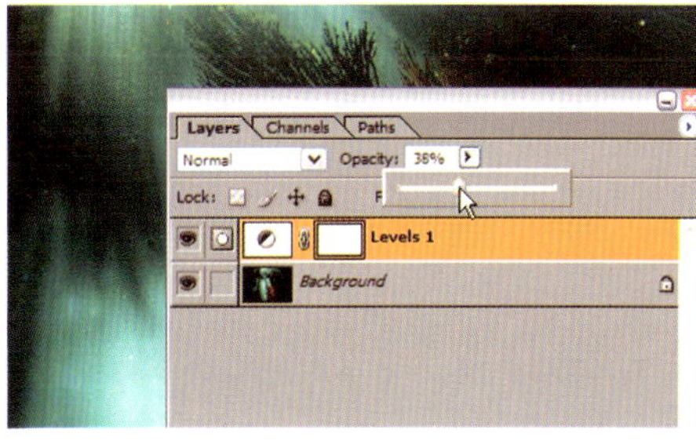

2. It should show 100%. Click on the arrow to display a slider.

3. Adjust the percentage by moving the slider: this allows you to reduce the effect of the adjustment layer created from 100% down to 0%. Very effective for subtle fine-tuning and far beyond any type of controls ever available in an old fashioned darkroom.

How to process difficult images using CURVES in Photoshop?

Adjustment with 'Curves' in Photoshop is an advanced technique which is used with problematic images that require very precise control over just a part of the brightness range. Much like the Levels, Curves precisely allows you to adjust the tonal range of an image. Comparatively, Levels is like a butcher's knife and Curves is more like a surgeon's scalpel in precision.

1. Click Layer > New Adjustment Layer and select Curves.

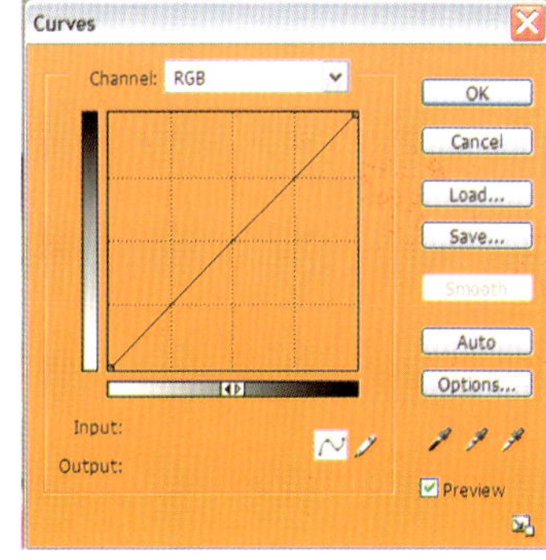

2. A New Layer window named Curves will appear. Click OK.

3. A Curves window appears.

4. The channel should be set to RGB.

The horizontal axis represents the original brightness values of the pixels (Input levels); the vertical axis is the new brightness levels (Output levels). For RGB images, Curves displays brightness values from 0 to 255, with the shadows on the left.

4. Make sure the preview box is checked so that you can see the changes as you make them.

5. Move your mouse which is now a crosshair cursor to point A and click to establish a drag point - this point will be used to adjust shadows. Move to point B, click and establish a mid-tone drag point. Move to point C and establish a highlight drag point.

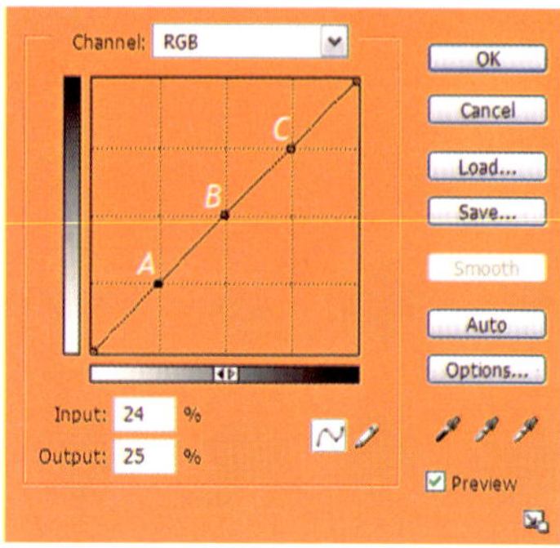

8. Move cursor to point A - the shadow drag point, click and pull it down or up slowly while watching the shadows in your image. Stop pulling when the image is to your liking. Most mid-tones and all the highlights should remain unchanged.

9. Move cursor to point C, the highlight drag point, click and push it up or down while watching the highlights in your image. Stop pushing when things have lightened to your liking. You can also move the drag point slightly left or right for more subtle tone changes.

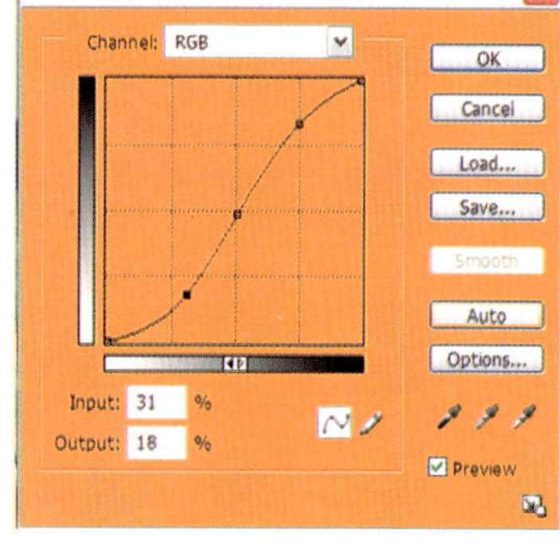

10. Move cursor to B, the mid-tone point and tweak it up or down so the overall image tonality looks good. This may not be required.

QUICK FIX

In order to make quick adjustments to the colour contrast and distribution without resorting to the more elaborate methods, use the black and white eyedroppers found in the 'Levels' or 'Curves' box: select the black or white eyedropper, move eyedropper over your picture area and click where you want area to be black or white. This can have dramatic results on pictures which simply lack contrast or have a colour cast.

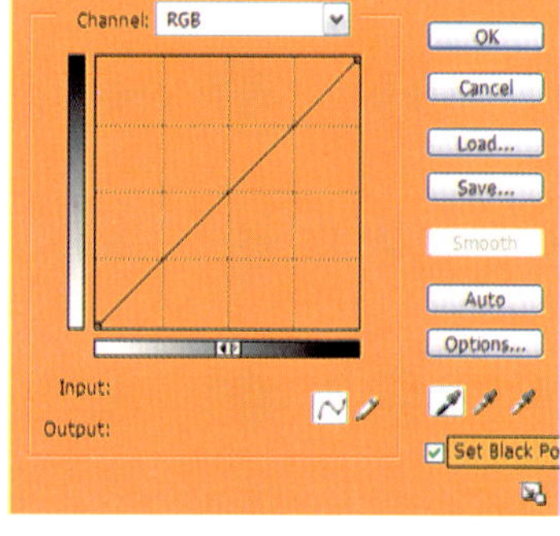

SHARPENING PICTURES - Sharpen Last

Digital cameras introduce a number of artefacts during the capturing and recording process. As such 90% of digital images require at least a minimal amount of sharpening. Restoring the sharpness is possible as long as the image is not grossly out of focus. The industry standard is to use the UNSHARP MASK (USM) filter in Photoshop.

By now you would have learned to use Adjustment Layers for enhancement in Photoshop. Adjustment Layers is not an option for Unsharp Masking – USM must be done to the original image. As such sharpening should be done last in the image enhancement process. Many professional photographers save their files without sharpening. USM is only applied when they are ready to use the image.

How to sharpen with Photoshop?

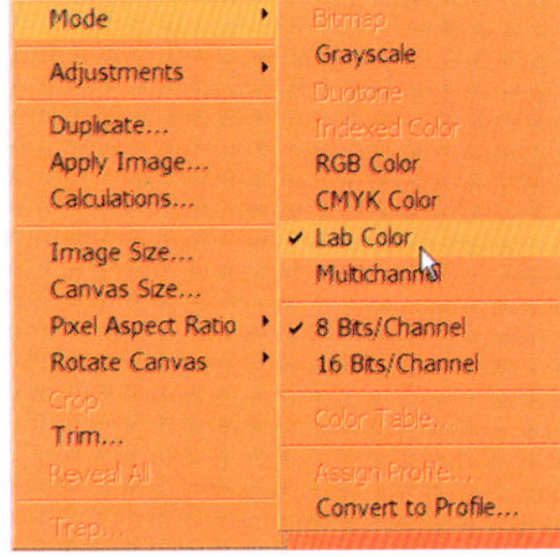

1. Start with Layers > Duplicate Layer – a Duplicate Layer will appear, with the name 'Background Copy'. Click OK. Make sure this layer is highlighted in the layer palette. Sharpening is done on this duplicate layer.

2. Go to Image > Mode > Lab Color: This method only affects the monochrome data and not the colour data. This leads to higher quality images and prints.

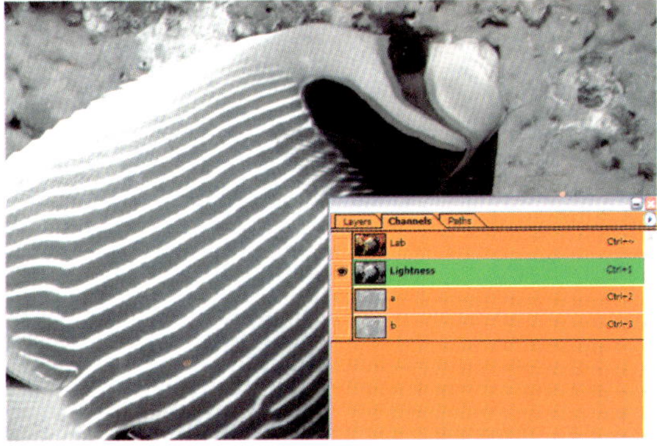

3. Go to View > Actual Pixel: this is the preferred option to see the sharpening process OR choose Fit on Screen, and see the Actual Pixels in the Unsharp Mask window.

4. Then click on Window > Show Channels. In the Channels palette select the Lightness channel – this channel will be highlighted and your image will be in grayscale.

6. Now choose Filter > Sharpen > Unsharp Mask. There are 3 sliders for the 3 parameters for sharpening: Amount: Radius: Threshold. A good all-round starting point is 125 / 1.5 / 1

• 'Radius' indicates how far around each pixel the software needs to look. The greater the radius the more out of focus the original picture, and the noisier the result. If a Radius greater than 3.5 is required, the picture is probably not sharp enough to achieve an acceptable result.

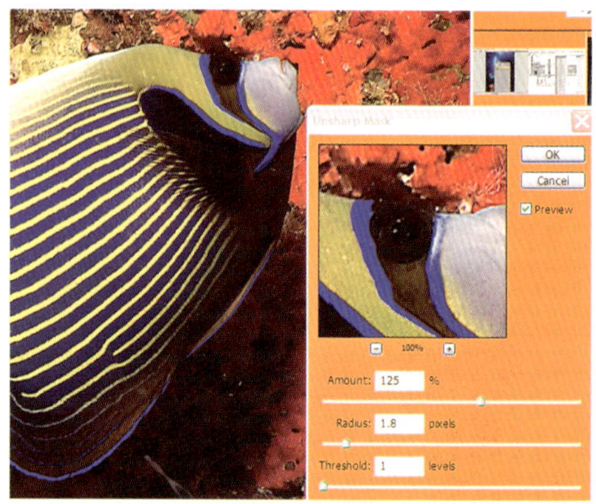

• 'Amount' tells the software how much sharpening needs to be applied. Start with 125 and move down or up, to a maximum of 250 if required. Progressively, increase the 'Radius' until you can obtain a visible effect on your picture. Decrease the 'Amount' until the picture looks natural.

• 'Threshold' tells the software how different adjacent points should be for the area to be sharpened. With 'Radius' and 'Amount', the software will sharpen areas of the pictures which you don't want sharpened (e.g. the blue sea in the background), resulting in visible noise in these areas. Progressively increase the 'Threshold' value, starting from 0, until you find the best compromise between sharpness and noise.

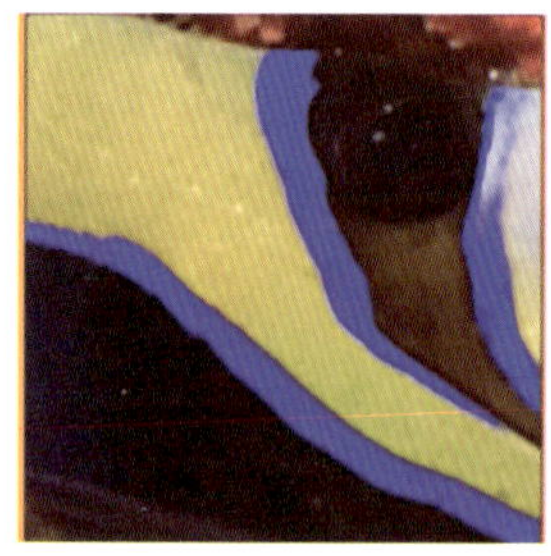

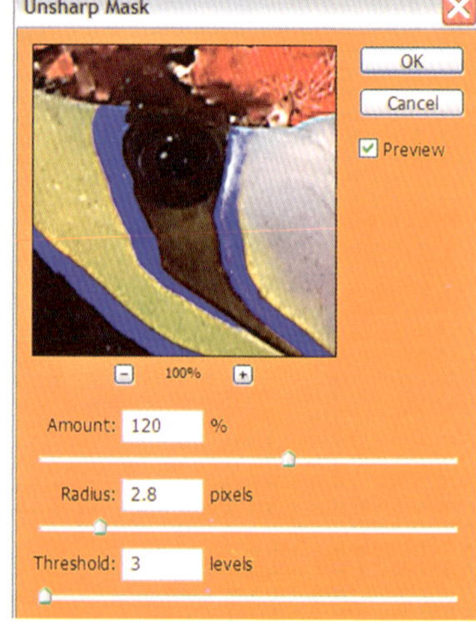

7. Click the 'Preview' button on and off to view the effect. Click OK to accept the sharpening.

8. Select Image > Mode > RGB Color to complete the sharpening process. In the layers palette highlight the Background layer – click the eye icon on and off to see the before and after process. You can also use the Opacity too on the top right hand corner to vary the sharpening percentage!

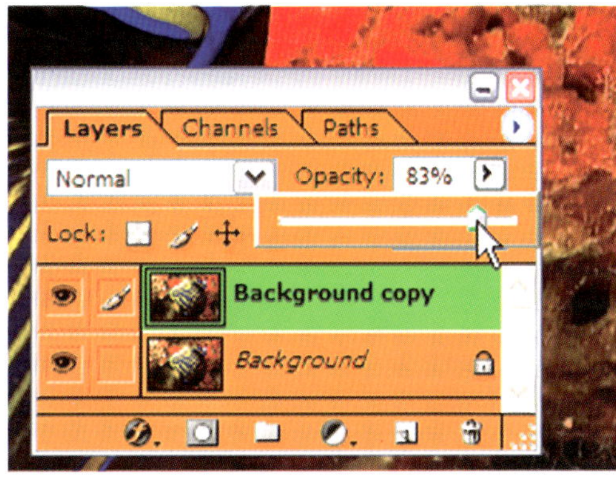

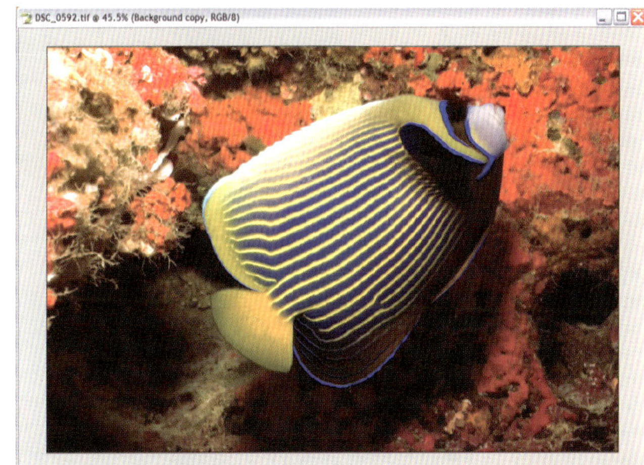

Before

HINT: Remember to make sure your file is saved as tiff - to preserve all layers. To send a file to a lab for printing, Resize as required, Flatten, Sharpen then save as TIFF format.

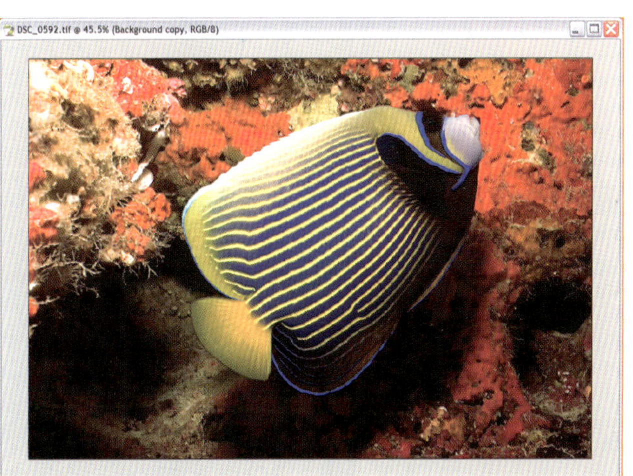

After

4/3 Printing Digital Pictures

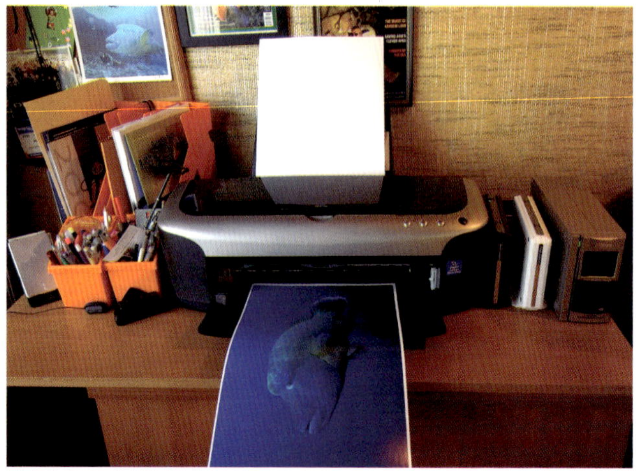

After extensive tests, we find that EPSON printers are best for the small office and home digital lab. For optimum reproduction use a calibrated and paper stock colour profile.

The simplest option is to drop a CD or memory card with the pictures you want printed to your local photo shop. However, the joy of digital photography is to print your own pictures. The best option is a photo inkjet printer with seven colour cartridges such as the Epson 2100 or equivalent. Use the best photo paper you can find and a good printing software, such as Epson's, which allows you to use your calibrated printer or paper profile. This is the most desirable option. Registered users of this book will be able to download from www.OceanEarthPictures.com for advanced printing tips.

Printing your pictures: size does matter

In order to get decent results when printing your pictures, you have to be aware of the size of the image, as well as the resolution of the printer.

Print quality is expressed in terms of resolution, expressed in dots per inch (dpi). Typically, the higher the resolution, the better the quality of the picture will be. 300 dpi is the industry standard though some printers work best with 200dpi. The minimum all round you should aim for is 200dpi. Below this resolution, the quality starts to visibly deteriorate.

Guide

A 5 megapixel camera produces 2560 x 1920 images, which at 200dpi will yield 12.8" wide by 9.6" high prints (32cm x 24cm).

A 2 megapixel camera that produces 1600 x 1200 images will only produce prints of 8" x 6" (20cm x 15cm) at 200 dpi.

How to print an 8" x 10" photo

1. Open the image in Photoshop. In the tool box, click on the Crop tool.

2. In the dialogue boxes at the top of the window, key in 10in for 'Width', 8in for 'Height' and 200 for 'Resolution'.

3. Click in the picture and drag to create the outline of the area you want to retain. The proportions of the selection will automatically be of the right dimensions.

4. When you are satisfied with your selection, click Enter.

5. For landscape pictures, you can simply click on the double arrow to invert the values of 'Width' and 'Height'.

6. Save the image with another name before printing.

7. Proceed to Print. In the Properties Window of your printer, choose no image enhancement, select the correct paper type, and if possible assign monitor or paper profiles.

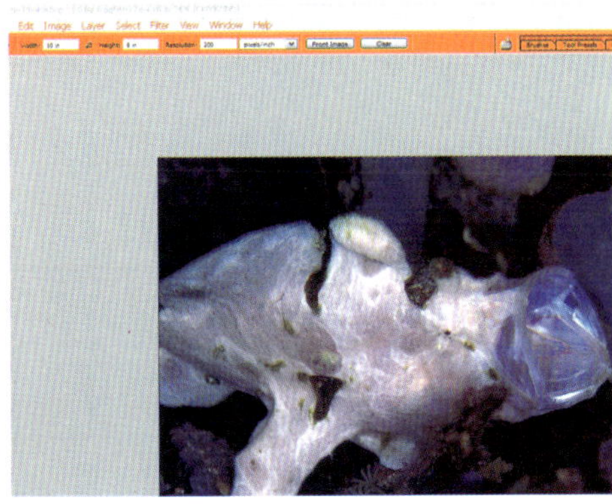

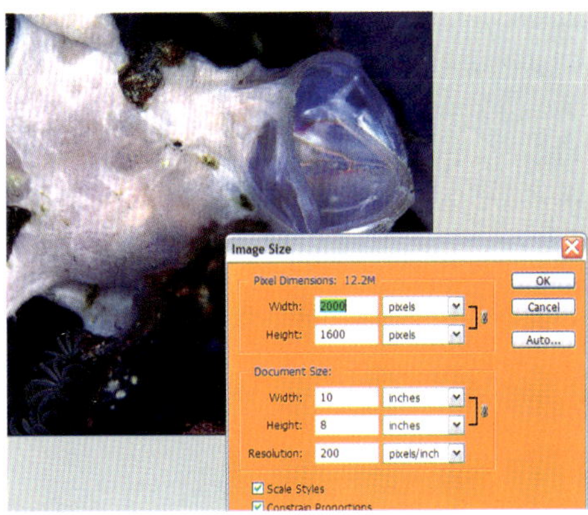

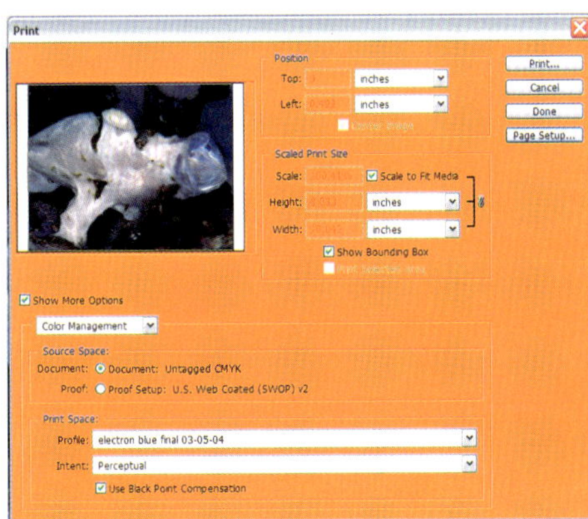

4/4 Managing Image Information, Preserving Copyright

One interesting thing with digital images is that they record certain information in addition to the picture itself. This includes the model of camera that was used, the original size of the picture, the aperture and shutter speed used, the focal length, ISO number and exposure compensation, etc. This is called the EXIF information of the picture. EXIF information is a very useful tool to analyse pictures when reviewing them on a computer.

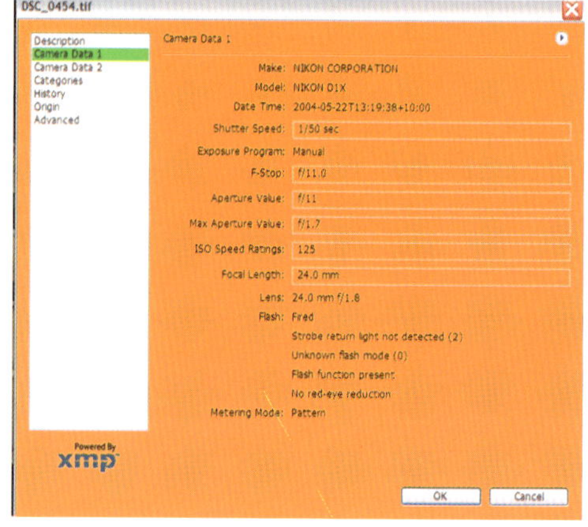

To access the EXIF information: Click File > File Info > Advanced within your image editing software. It is found under the 'EXIF Properties', 'Camera Data' or 'Metadata' headings.

Other information that can be recorded in this EXIF header is the author and title of the picture. If you intend to publish your pictures, online or otherwise, it is a good idea to assert your rights. The first option is to add a visible watermark to your picture.

In Photoshop: Use the 'Horizontal Type' tool by pressing 'T', and add in the copyright status, notice and your name, year etc. Select White as default text colour.

Go to Layers palette, highlight the text layer – use the Opacity tool on the top right hand corner and reduce visibility to 50% This is a simple method, it may be bypassed by clever image editing, but it serves as a useful deterent. For online images, keep image size to 50k – this restricts commercial usefulness to potential thieves.

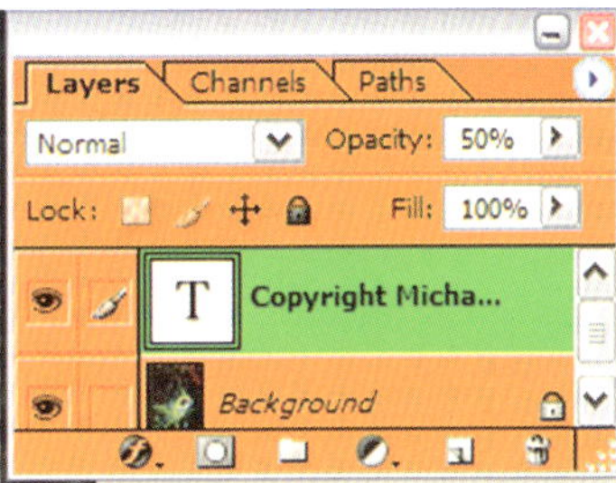

Another option is to use an invisible digital watermark, which is a paid service. You can register with www. digimarc.com. This places certain information within the picture file, such as your name and email address. The cost of registration is relatively minimal if you are going to publish a small number of pictures (US$49 for 1,000 pictures) on line. The watermark is invisible, and will resist a number of editing processes, including format conversions.

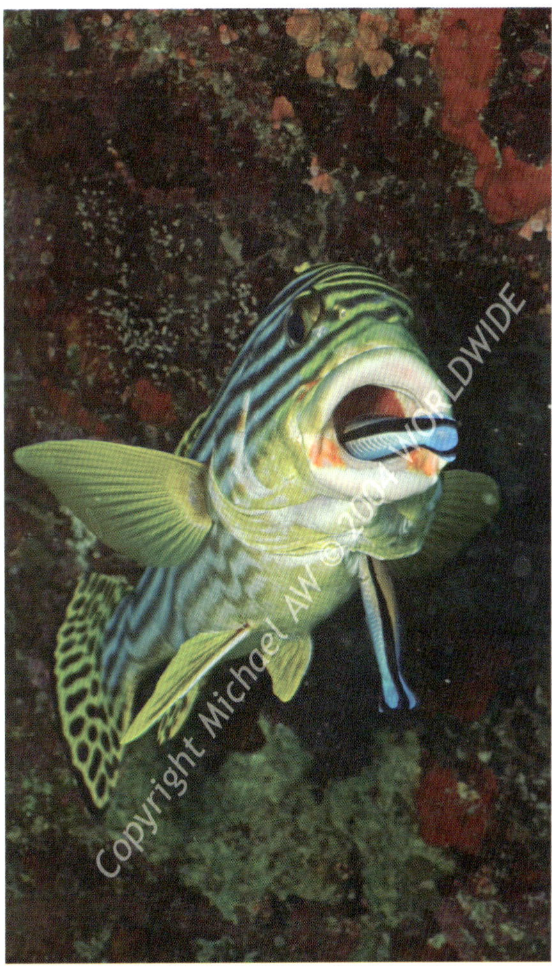

Module Five
Beyond the Basics

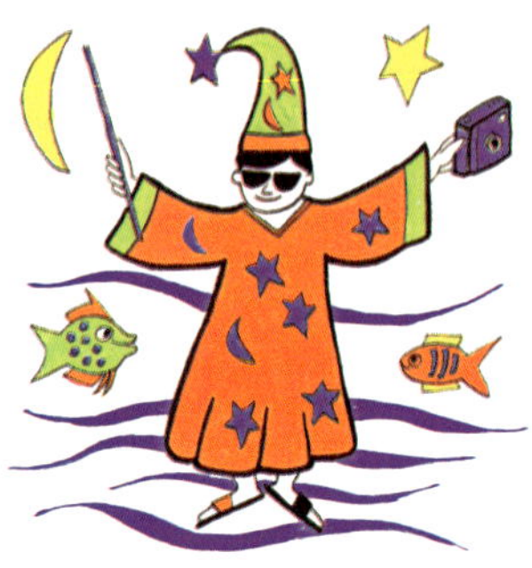

5/1 TOP TEN Classic Masterpieces to Emulate

Here are 10 all time successful compositions that you can try to imitate. These images have been published in glossy magazines or have won awards at photographic competitions. The techniques and secrets behind the images are revealed here. Simply try to use similar equipment, go to the same location, apply the same setting, and shoot to heart content. Make it an assignment to re-create the images and soon you will be creating your own works of art. You may choose to send us your images for review: review@underwaterartists.com

The masterpieces in this portfolio are captured with a wide range of digital cameras and housings – from the simplest consumer camera to professional DSLRs. Whilst there is subtle difference in optical quality they are a representation of the results you will be able to achieve with digital cameras. You will also notice they are easy to find subjects and they are popular even among professional underwater photographers.

Spot On – MATHIEU MEUR

Bunaken Marine Park, Manado, Indonesia
Camera: Nikon Coolpix 5000, AQUATICA housing
Strobe: Ikelite DS125 @ 1/4 power **Exposure:** f7.6, 1/125 sec, ISO 100

Long Nose hawkfish are the graduation subject – the fish that you will attempt to shoot once you feel that you have a grasp of the basics. They are really not difficult as they do momentarily stop to rest and they are quite like to look at you. The eye of this model is smartly positioned on a vital intersection of the RULE OF THIRDS grid.

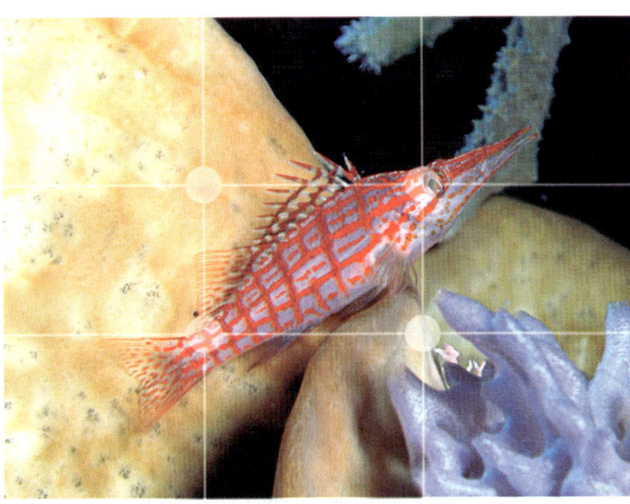

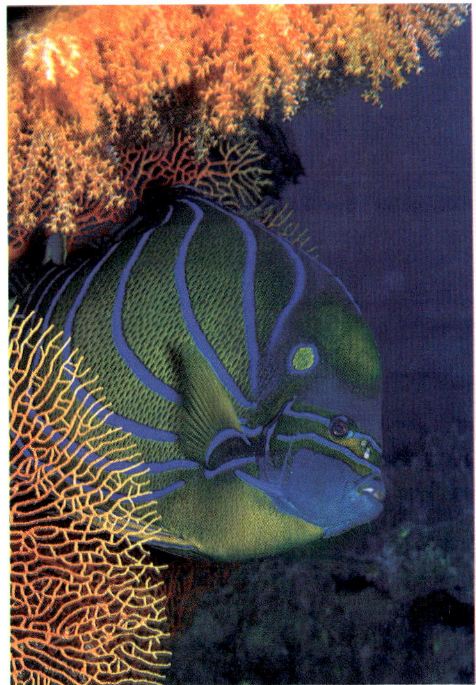

Angelfish portrait –
MICHAEL AW

Miri, Sarawak, Malaysia
Camera: Nikon D1X, Nikkor 60mm 2.8, SEACAM housing
Strobe: single Ikelite S200 @ 1/2 power
Exposure: f11, 1/60 sec, EV-1, ISO 125

Angelfishes are fond of swimming beneath overhangs. Once you spot them, move in slowly. Let them come to you. It is only a matter of time, they are curious.

WOW! –SHERELLE FARRINGTON

Paradise Pier, Nth Sulawesi
Camera: Olympus C5050Z
Strobe: single 1/2 power,
Exposure: f8, 1/2000 sec, ISO 64,

Caught with mouth open! This *Antennarius commersonii* – Giant frogfish is possibly telling Sherelle to back off by showing her that his mouth is big enough to swallow her.

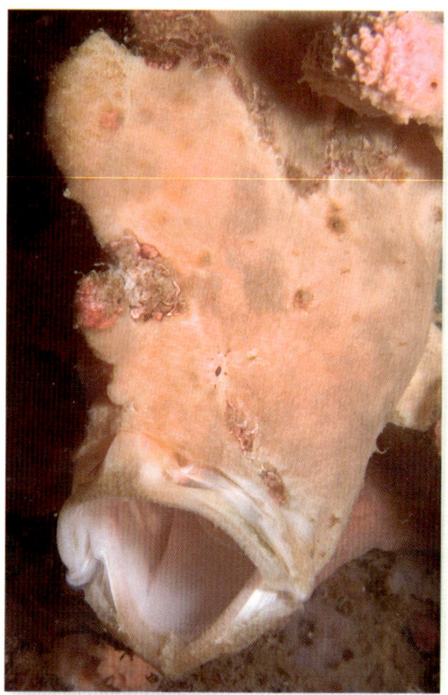

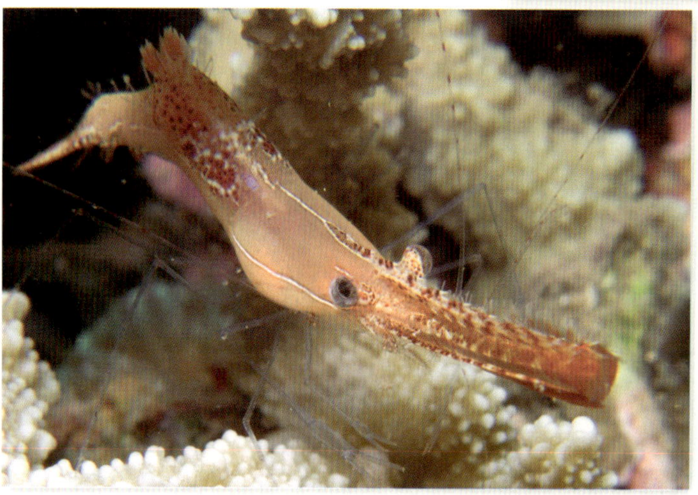

QUACKY shrimp –SHERELLE FARRINGTON

Mori Reef, Nth Sulawesi
Camera: Olympus C5050Z Strobe: single 1/4 power,
Exposure: f8, 1/2000 sec, ISO 64, Macro lens x 2 attachment
This cryptic Plumed shrimp (*Leander plumosus*) comes out to feed at night, hopping among coral colonies – a fair bit of patience is required to capture this animal.

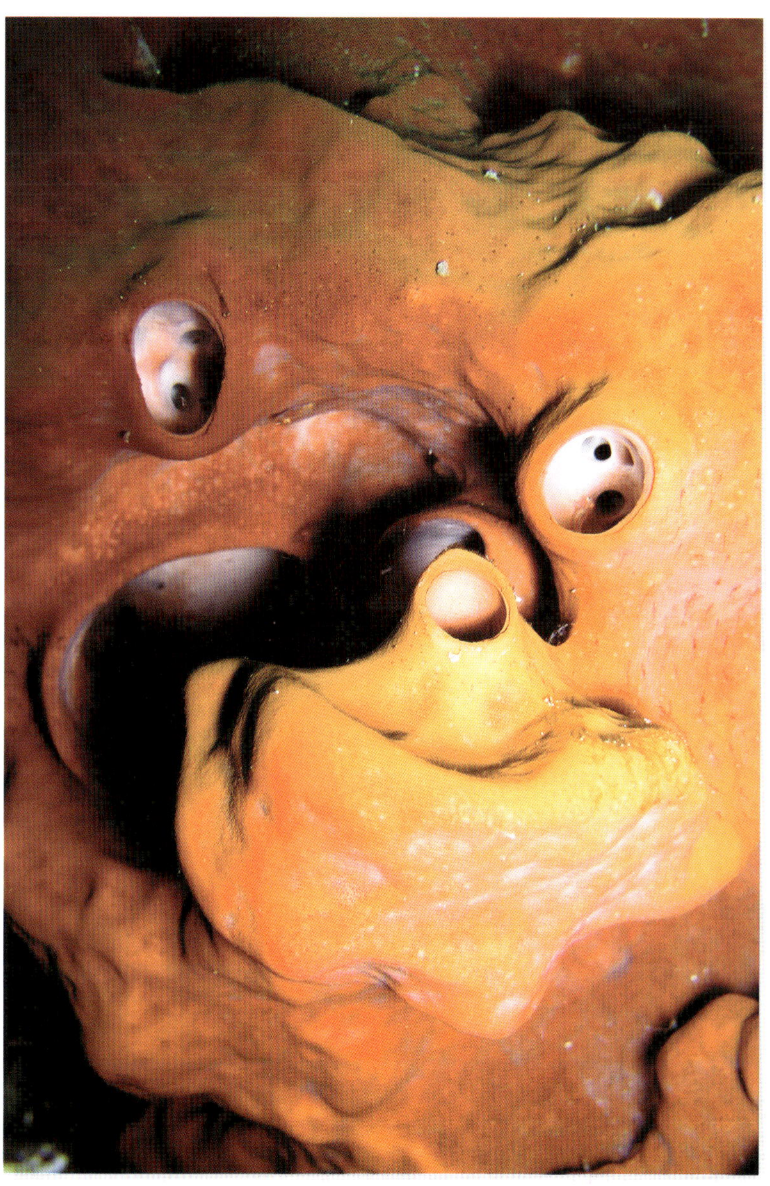

Brother Bear – LIM YEW BENG

Bunaken Marine Park, Manado, Indonesia
Camera: Olympus C5050Z **Strobe:** Internal
Exposure: f3.2, 1/640 sec, ISO 64
Sponges are everywhere and they deserve more attention. Use your imagination, open your eyes and you will see many interesting 'sculptures' like this massive sedentary sponge.

Irian Morning –
Cassandra Dragon

Raja Ampat, Irian, Indonesia
Camera: Olympus 5050Z
Strobe: single Ikelite S 50 with custom diffuser
Exposure: f2.8, 1/800 sec, EV -0.1, ISO 64

The passage between the island of Wageo and Gam are coral outcrops, sea fans - the walls along the channel are covered in entirety with lush, colourful soft corals. The morning light reveals a surrealistic landscape.

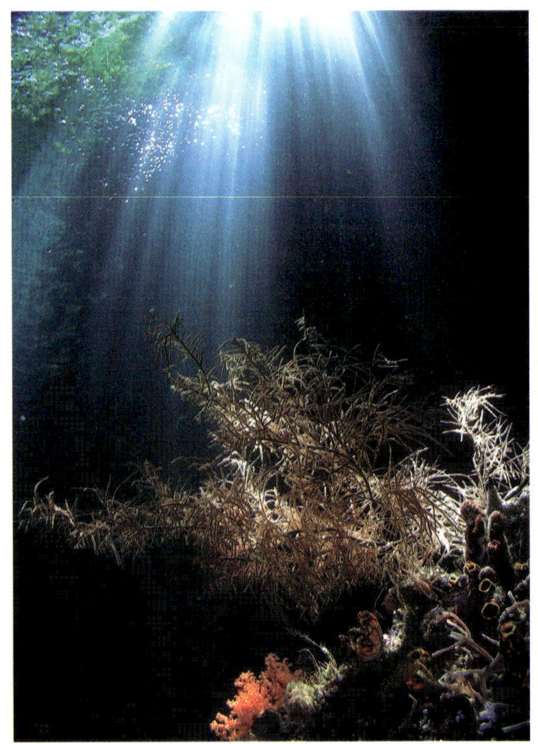

2 horsepower – Sherelle Farrington

Raja Ampat, Irian, Indonesia
Camera: Olympus 5050Z
Strobe: Sea & Sea 90 strobe *Exposure:* f2.8, 1/800 sec, EV -0.1, ISO 64

One of the finest shots of Hippocampus bargibanti ever captured - they are little rascals with skins and textures that matches the sea fan to which they live. They are one of the most popular but difficult subjects to manage.

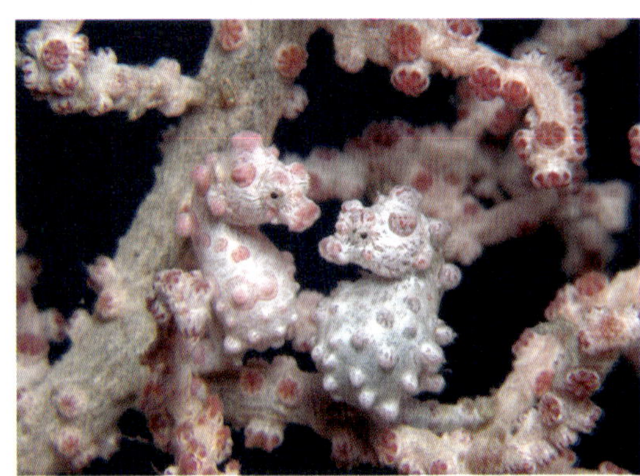

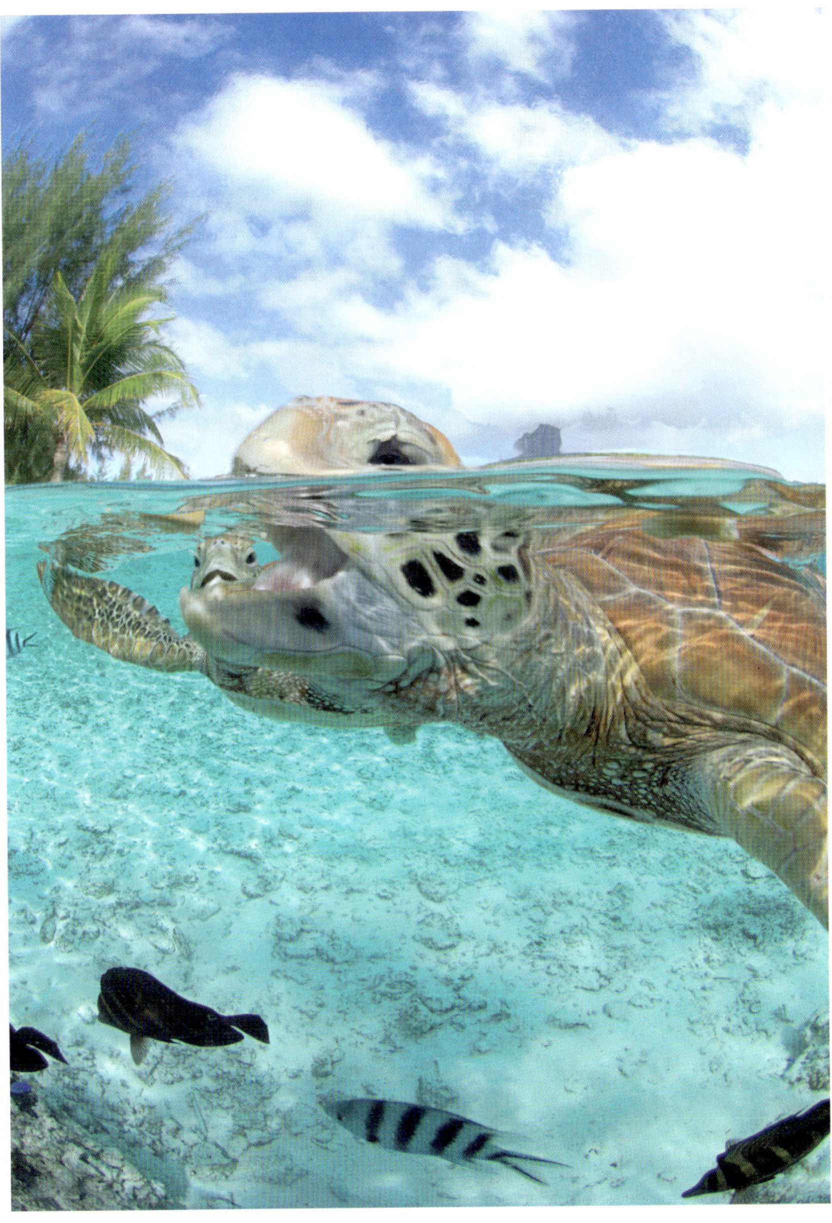

Out of Breath – MICHAEL AW

Bora Bora, French Polynesia
Camera: Nikon D2X, Seacam housing; Natural light
Exposure: f11, 1/100 sec, ISO 125
I was determined to get and over and under image of a turtle -
took me 4 hours following a few turtles to get this one frame!

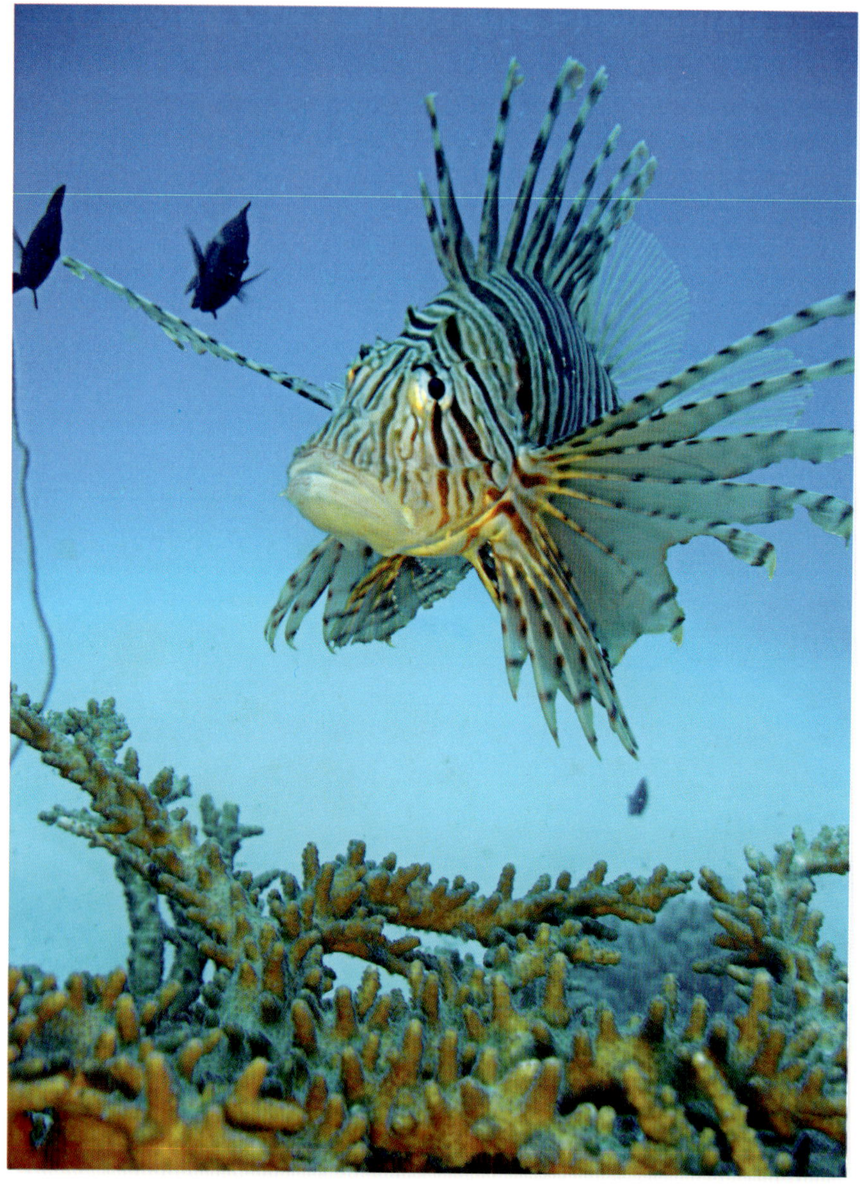

Lionfly – MICHAEL AW

Redang, Malaysia

Camera: Sony P100 **Strobe:** Ikelite S50, Manual Control @ 1/4 power

Exposure: f5, 1/125 sec, ISO 100

Another usual suspect on the reef – but you will have to find one that is fond of hovering in the water column during the day. I waited for this one to turn its face towards me.

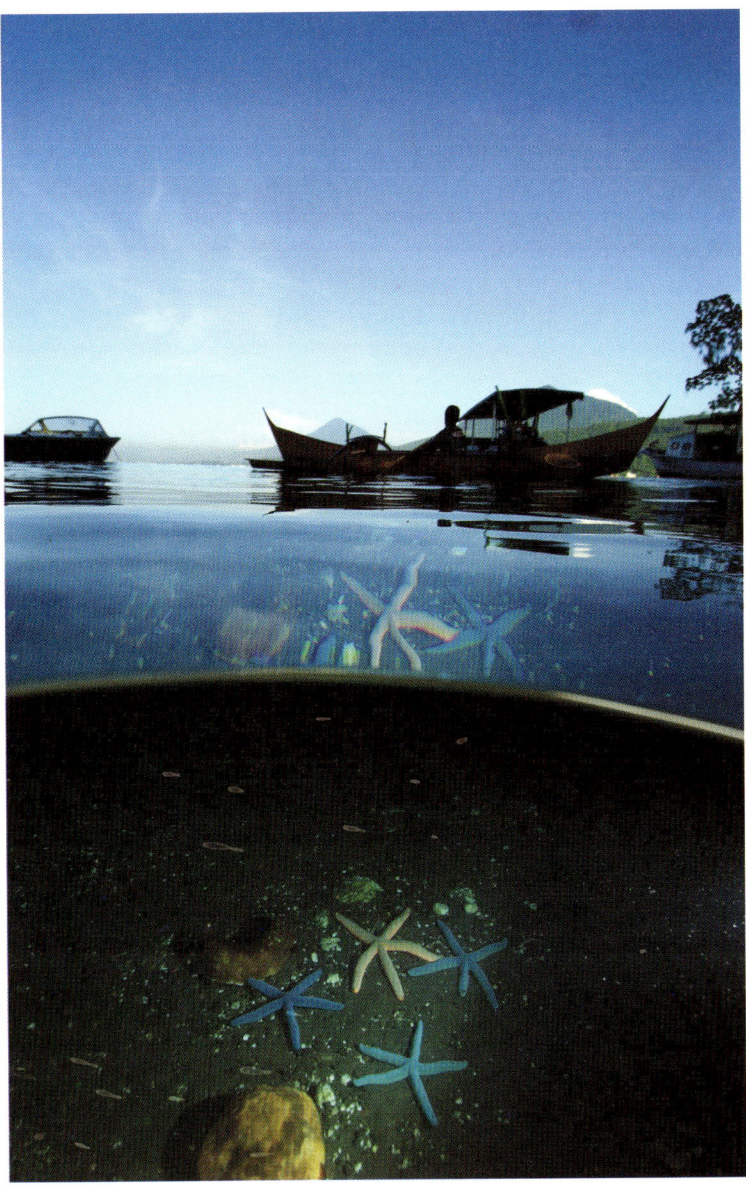

The Ultimate Challenge

With this guide, we hope you will learn the basics of the art and science of digital photography. Though duplicating composition is a proven way to learn, the idea is not yours. Learn to create by experimenting with light, composition and with varying techniques. Learn to shoot from another perspective. By doing this it will free you from the chains of conformity and you will start to create pictures that no one else has ever seen before.

5/2 Shooting with HMI Lights

For a different feel and rendition to underwater imagery, the use of a HMI light source is a great alternative. Watt for watt, Hydragyrum Medium arc-length Iodide (HMI) lights are two to four times brighter than their tungsten equivalents. The main advantage for digital photography is apparent. With a DSLR camera capable of firing 3 to 6 frames per second, there are no underwater strobes capable of recycling to keep up with the camera firing speed. HMIs light source have a "daylight" colour temperature around 5,600 degrees K, similar to natural sunlight. Light produced by HMIs has a higher colour temperature (longer light wavelengths), and thus penetrates further, providing greater true-colour illumination over a wide area, seemingly able to "wrap around" the subject, enhancing depth and softening shadows.

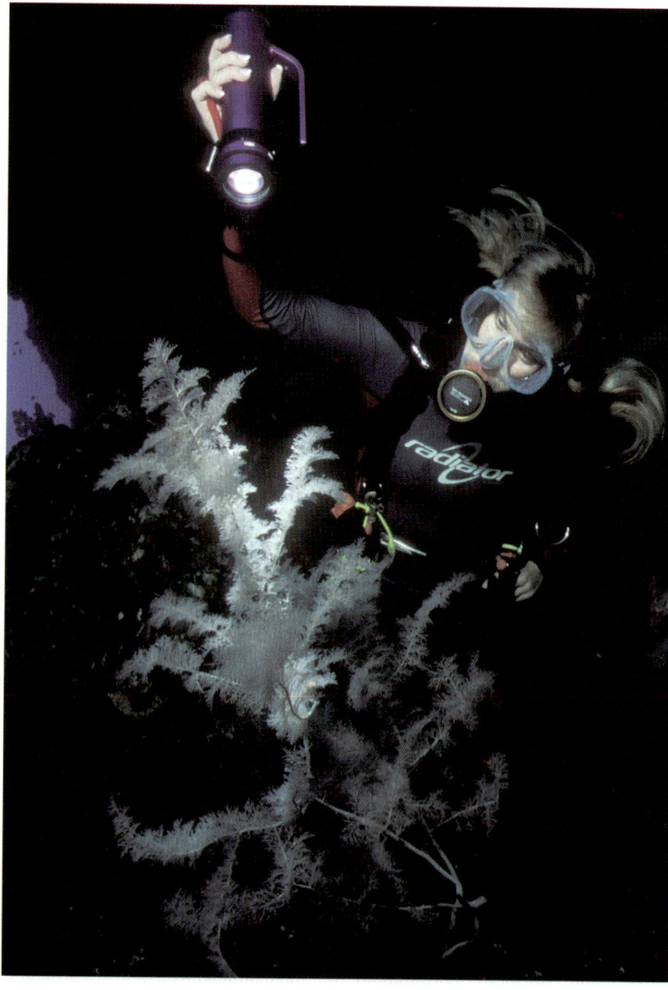

In this image, the HMI is used as a highlight to illuminate the white coral tree, the model is lit with an Ikelite S200 at 1/4 power

Keeping unnecessary light out between the object and the camera reduces the illumination of undesired back scatter. By strategically placing a couple of small HMI lights closer to the subject with continuous illumination back scatter problems are greatly reduced. For the purpose of close-up photography, it is necessary to use units rated 24w and above. Invest in a reliable unit such as the Keldan Solaris Pro – specially fitted with a diffuser for photographic applications.

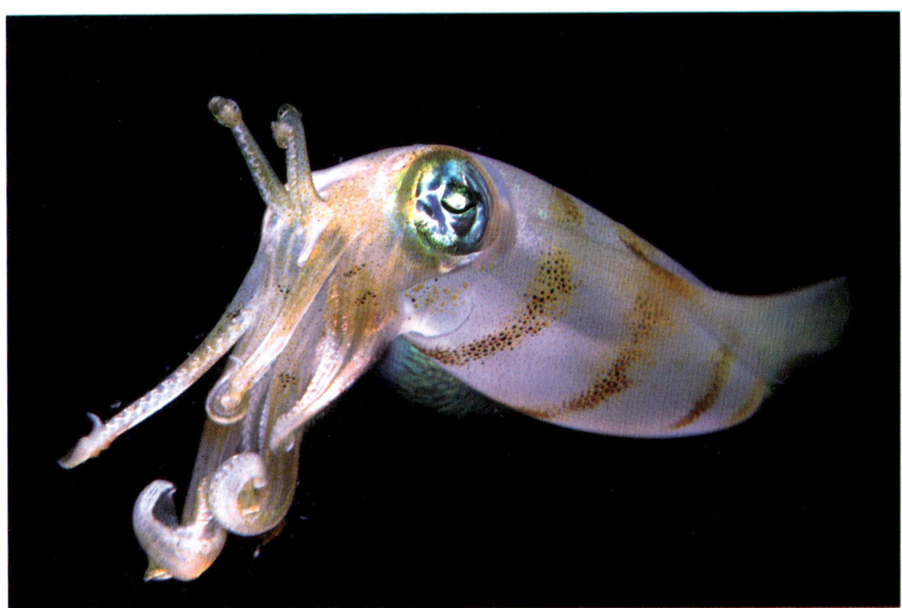

I shot non-stop over 180 frames in 20 minutes of this very obliging squid with a 24 w KELDAN SOLARIS PRO HMI - a flash unit would not have recycled fast enough.

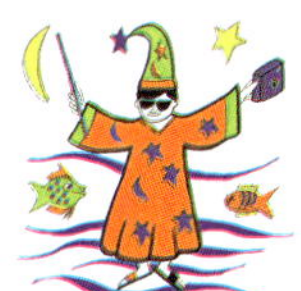

How to Use HMI lights

1. For DSLR set ISO to 400 and for Prosumer camera, set to the highest possible.
2. Use S priority and set speed at 1/90 second or higher.
3. If your HMI unit offers variable power settings, use the lower option.
4. Position HMI light in front of lens pointing downward to subject at a 45° angle.
5. Start with shooting macro at distant of 30cm, using f16 aperture – bracket up or down for optimum exposure.

5/3 Shooting with Filters

Shooting with filters presents an attractive alternative to the traditional natural light / external strobes combination. The results can be striking, with a more even light spread across the pictures as compared to scenes lit with strobes. This gives pictures a feel that is closer to what divers actually see underwater.

How to shoot with filters:

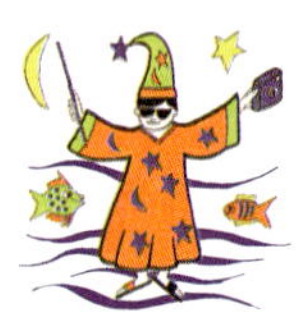

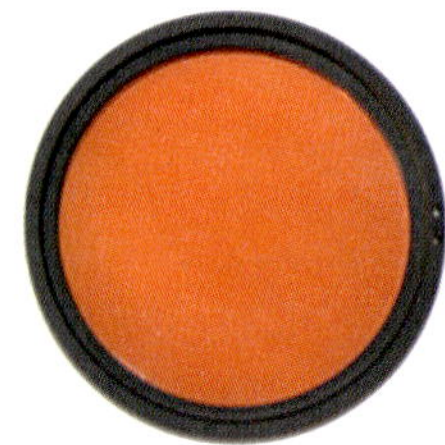

Red filter - 10 BAR

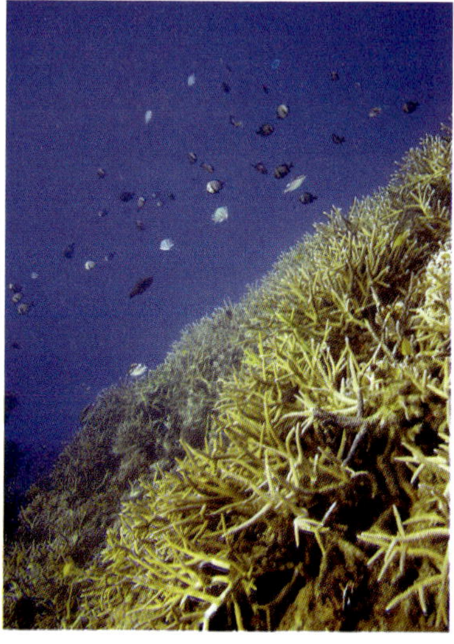

1. Select a filter that's adapted to the colour of water: red for blue tropical waters, and magenta for green temperate waters. This can be used in combination with a colour-warming filter. For DSLR users, it is also possible to use a "Magic Filter", which is specifically designed for underwater use.

2. The filter is generally fitted onto the outside of the housing port for a consumer camera, and directly onto the lens for a DSLR.

3. In order to take full advantage of the filter, you must make a custom white balance while underwater (refer to your camera manual on how this is done on your particular model). This can be done on any part of the reef with neutral colours, on a white slate, on the sand, or even your hand.

4. When shooting with filters, the sun should be behind you, lighting your subject.

5. Shoot with a slightly downward angle to obtain a nice gradation of the background water.

HINTS

• Even with good water clarity, filters are effective up to a depth of about 15 metres. There is just not enough ambient light at deeper depths to allow for desirable results.

• Redo the custom white balance often, say every time you change depth by more than 2 metres, to get better results and minimise post-processing.

5/4 Recovering Pictures

Memory cards and hard drives are not fail-safe. In fact, it is generally a matter of when, not if they fail. When the worst happens, it is generally possible to recover some, if not all, of the pictures on the card using specialised software. Some programs, such as "Digital Photo Recovery" or "Lexar Media Image Rescue", even allow you to restore pictures from cards that have been completely erased or formatted.

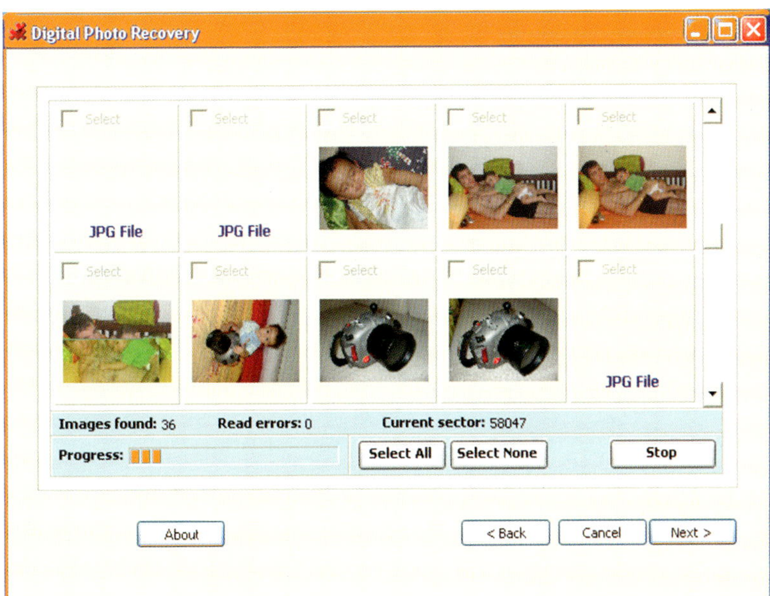

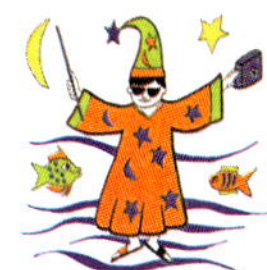

How to recover pictures:

The procedure is quite straightforward, and does not vary much from one program to another.

1. Place the affected card into a card reader attached to your computer.

2. Launch the recovery software

3. At this point you may need to select a few options – where to place the recovered photo, whether there are any particular image names that you are attempting to recover, etc.

4. Just press start and wait for the software to weave its magic!

More image recovery programmes at:
www.lexar.com/software/image_rescue.html
www.photosrecovery.com

5/5 Fast Track to Success

The most effective way to progress in photography is to be critiqued and judged by professionals in the industry. As photographers we are sometimes too close to our images to be objective. With constructive criticism we learn to see how viewers interpret our images. Here are a few ways to fast track your learning curve.

Photo Competitions

1. There are many photo competitions run by private clubs and organisations, magazines, manufacturers and film festivals. Don't just compete for the smaller club competitions – go for the big ones.

2. Though initially you may not have any success, make it a point to view the winners – critique the winning images against yours. Write to the organisers for the scoring – they may not reveal the scores but may let you know how you fared against the top ten winners.

3. Don't be disheartened if you don't win – send the same images to another competition – different competition, different judges, different competitors.

4. If you know any professionals – show them ten of your best pictures and ask them for a honest opinion – sometimes the truth hurts, but it is the only way to learn.

5. Participate in Photo competitions – make sure that you read the rules and conditions carefully – pay attention especially to the criteria for the category that you choose to compete.

Hints on selecting images for competitions

1. First consider images that are technically correct – pay attention to exposure, backscatter and sharpness.

2. Composition – is the image well composed? Is the image balanced and pleasing to the eyes? Most competitions allow you to crop; do that to improve the submission.

3. WOW factor – this is perhaps the most important aspect; on first sighting – does the image have a WOW factor?

4. Narrow down your selection to four or five images – seek opinions from family and friends to select the final three.

5. Pay attention to past winners; these will give you an idea on the standard of the competitions and the competitors. Avoid submitting similar images of the previous years winner. Judges are constantly on the look out for new subjects or common subjects presented in a different way.

Participating in a photo trip or workshop with a working photographer is without a doubt the most effective way to fast track your skills in underwater photography. Normally hosted over a five to seven day period, the structure of a photo trip or workshop provides valuable hands on experience – learn from your mistakes and improve your images on site. This is an opportunity to meet fellow beginners and advanced shooters and learn from a team of professional photographers and industry experts. Often demo equipment is provided with professional assistance and critiques, and hands-on workshops. The Digital Download events hosted by Scuba Diver Australasia are structured to communicate both capture and workflow issues. The seminars and competitions are always rich with prizes and information that will take you to a competitive level of photography. Industry professionals are on site to give talks specifically targeted to the art and science of digital photography. For updated shoot out events – check out at www.michaelaw.com, www.scubadiveraustralasia.com

**Check out
BEYOND the
Ordinary PHOTO &
Naturalist Tour
www.michaelaw.com**

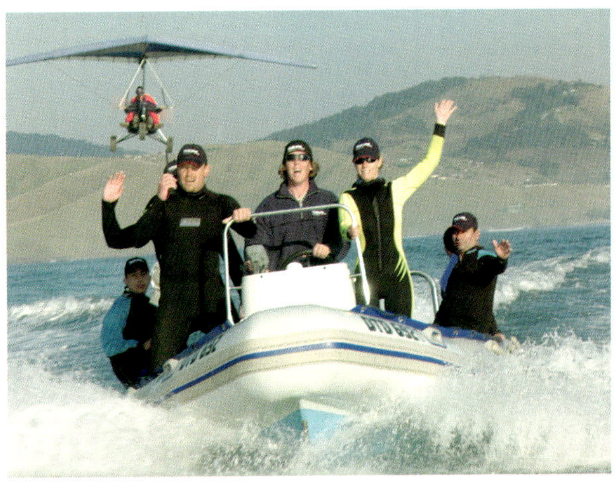

Recommended Web Resources
www.celebratethesea.com
www.divephotoguide.com
www.epicphotocontest.org
www.photoshowpiece.com
www.underwaterphotography.com
www.uwpmag.com
www.wetpixel.com

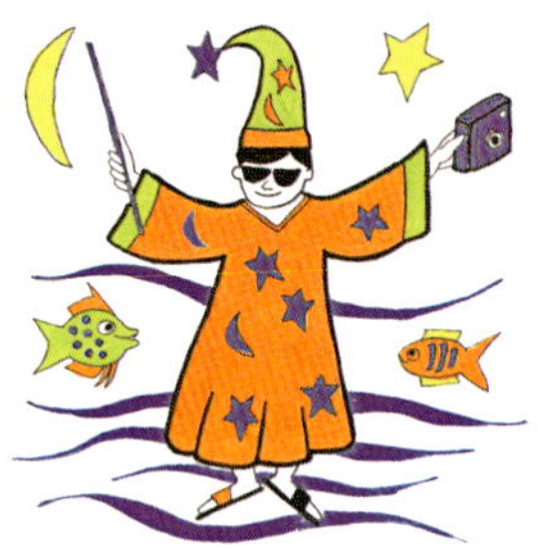

KNOWLEDGE REVIEW Module 1

1. To achieve a brighter picture, shall we use a large aperture – f2.8 or a small aperture – f16?

2. In digital photography, what is the definition of shutter speed?

3. List the 3 main advantages of a CCD sensor as compared to a CMOS sensor.

4. Shooting in A Mode allows you to control two important elements – what are they?

5. For Con/Prosumer users, what is the advantage for shooting in S-Mode.

6. What f-stop and shutter speed will you use for a lighter blue background.

7. How will you conduct a battery check on your camera effectively before a dive?

8. What is the most important exercise to conduct when using a new or a new second hand camera housing?

9. What is your first action when you suddenly see bubbles coming out of your housing during a dive?

10. List three essential equipment items for your camera tool box.

KNOWLEDGE REVIEW Module 2

1. In underwater photography, how will the sun affect your picture if it is coming from your back?

2. In relation to underwater strobes, what does a high guide number mean?

3. When shooting macro, how should you position your strobe to avoid backscatter?

4. When shooting wide angle with two strobes, how should you position them to avoid backscatter?

5. What kind of arms are best for underwater photography?

6. What are the three options for bracketing exposure?
7. What kind of lighting techniques will you use for wide angle photography?
8. What causes underexposed images?
9. What kind of flash will not work properly for digital photography underwater?
10. What is the advantage of adding a diffuser to your strobe?

KNOWLEDGE REVIEW Module 3

1. What are the most important elements in composition?
2. What is the principle guideline for macro pictures?
3. Why it is beneficial to vary the orientation of your picture?
4. Define the rule of thirds.
5. Why is the use of negative space an important consideration?
6. What are directional lines?
7. How will you use a model in your composition?
8. DSLR users - What is the most important criteria for a macro lens?
9. What can help bring out or emphasize a dominant element.
10. How much space in the frame should your subject occupy in order to be adequately conspicuous as the main subject?

KNOWLEDGE REVIEW Module 4

1. Why are JPEG images 'lossy'?
2. What kind of layers should you use for compensating exposure?
3. What kind of layer should you use for compensating sharpness?
4. Why is sharpening done last?
5. What kind of colour should you use for sharpening?
6. What does it mean when the picture histogram is concentrated around the centre, with almost nothing on the left and right sides?
7. What does it mean when the whole histogram is shifted towards the left, with almost nothing left on the right hand side?
8. Which filter will you use to sharpen images?
9. What are tools used by film photographers to enhance their pictures?
10. If you are to print your picture using an ink jet printer, what is the minimum resolution you should use?

To send Knowledge Reviews for certification, you have to register for membership at www.oceanearthpictures.com

More Digital Terminology

Blooming – A visual effect caused by overexposing a CCD to too much light, This "digital overexposure" can cause distortions of the image.

Calibration – The act of adjusting the colour of one device relative to another, such as a monitor to a printer. It is the process of adjusting the colour of one device to some established standard.

Chromatic Aberration – Also known as the "purple fringe effect." It is common in two Megapixel and higher resolution digital cameras when a dark area is surrounded by a highlight. Along the edge between dark and light you will see a line or two of purple or violet coloured pixels that shouldn't be there.

DPI – Dots per Inch. A measurement value used to describe either the resolution of a display screen or the output resolution of a printer.

Interpolated – Software programs can enlarge image resolution beyond the actual resolution by adding extra pixels using complex mathematic calculations.

Saturation – The degree to which a colour is undiluted by white light. If a colour is 100 percent saturated, it contains no white light. If a colour has no saturation, it is a shade of gray.

TIFF – Tagged Image File Format – An uncompressed image file format that is lossless.

White Balance – Refers to adjusting the relative brightness of the red, green and blue components so that the brightest object in the image appears white.

IMPORTANT REMINDER

1. Detailed Preparation: allow plenty of Time – remember the golden rule – ONE hour before dive for camera preparation and that is not including toilet stop! Pay close attention to all pieces of your photo equipment - use O-ring grease but sparingly, check all strobes fire, batteries are 100% - especially the camera battery.

2. Leads to Leaks – It only takes one fine fluff, one grain of sand, one strand of hair to break the O-ring seal and breach the seal integrity – install sync cords precisely – this connection is prone to flooding. Install slowly and carefully.

3. Water Check – have camera system checked and handed over to you – do not dive in with your system. Once system is handed over to you, secure the system with a lanyard.

4. Diving Equipment – cameras do not provide you with air underwater – you need to check your diving equipment too. Be considerate to non photographers. Do not hold up a dive while you prepare your kit: Have everything ready to go, all systems checked well before dive time.

5. Read, practise and learn with this guide. Remember: "Failure can be avoided with preparation. With preparation, you will be prepared for success". You have to be prepared for that 'Lucky Shot'.

Recommended Reference Books by the Same Author

If you are now venturing into underwater digital photography you can immerse yourself in some lavish beautiful books of the sea. With our collection, you can just about indulge in almost every aspect of underwater photography. These recommended high quality books and handbooks offer a true wealth of knowledge in composition, real life experiences and most importantly awareness of the behaviour of fishes and invertebrates – where they live, what they eat, when they sleep, mate and play. Of course in these books are tips on how to photograph them as well.

To order: one@oneocean.com / www.michaelaw.com

RICHEST REEFS - Michael AW

Richest Reefs is illustrated by some of the most beautiful images of the sea, showing off the richest reefs of the Indonesian Archipelago. There are old images, new images and many award winning ones from Bunaken, Lembeh Strait, Togeans, Bali, Komodo Alor, Tukang Besi and the most recent wonder, Raja Ampat, Papua, rated by leading marine scientists as the most valuable cluster of reefs in the world. 168 pages, case bound printed using six-colour printing technology on 150 gsm matt art paper in a generous 280cm x 260cm format.

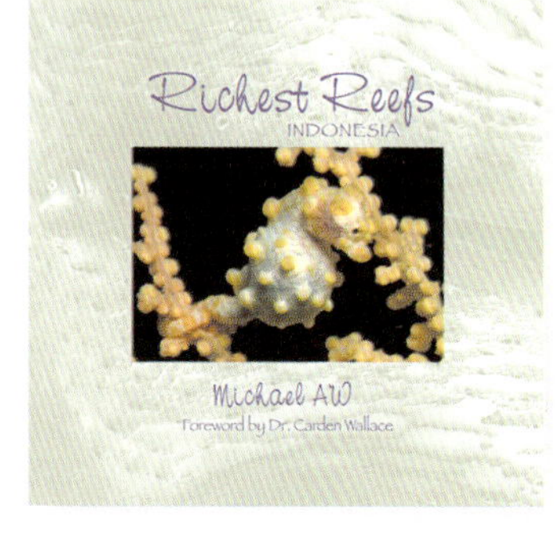

Celebrate the Sea – Michael AW / Stephen Wong

Celebrate the Sea – is the hallmark of all beautiful books of our seas. Using 6-colour printing technology the book is printed on fine matt art 155 gsm paper in a generous 275mm x 273mm – 180 pages format.

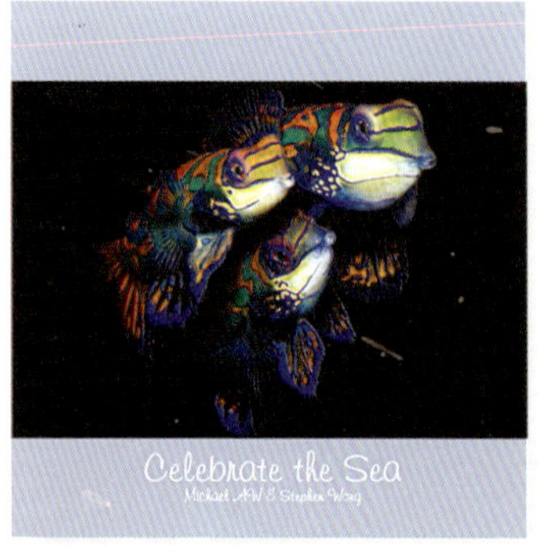

Raves by Stan Waterman

'Two internationally acclaimed underwater photographers and writers have joined to produce a most impressive and excellent coffee table collection of underwater images. It is entitled "Celebrate the Sea", by Michael Aw and Stephen Wong. Both diver/photographers are thorough professionals with too many awards in international competitions to list. The macro photography is stunning. The range of images profits from their major area of diving in the Western Pacific where numbers of species, weird and beautiful marine animals proliferate. Michael Aw is the publisher/editor of ASIAN GEOGRAPHIC and SCUBA DIVER magazines. His accompanying texts for the visual images in "Celebrate the Sea" are personally engaging, succinct and often poetic. Environmental concerns for the sea are a strong motif that underlies the fine text. An eloquent, two-page "Appreciation" by David Doubilet starts the reader's journey through this definitely superior new book.'
Stan Waterman 18 May 2002

Tropical Reef Fishes:

A handy 'getting to know' learning and identification guide for reef fishes in 3 colour coded segments - easy, simple and straightforward. Get acquainted with reef fishes, where they live, how they live, what they eat plus all the lucid secrets of sex in the sea. Tropical Reef Fishes takes you beyond the academia, translating scientific jargon into laymans language. Over 500 sharp colourful pictures, supported by concise informative descriptions indicating distribution, size, common and scientific names, habitat and exposure details. - 160 pages

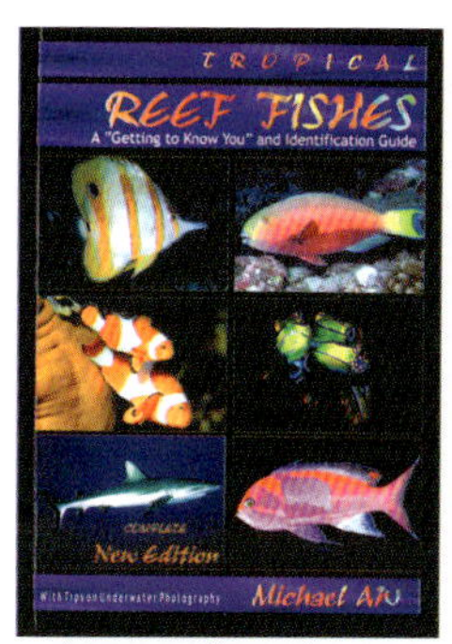

Tropical Reef Life:

An in-depth marine awareness and identification guide for hard and soft corals, crustaceans, molluscs, worms, anemones, echinoderms and ascidians. Over 500 pictures with tips for photographer. 160 pages over 550 pictures.

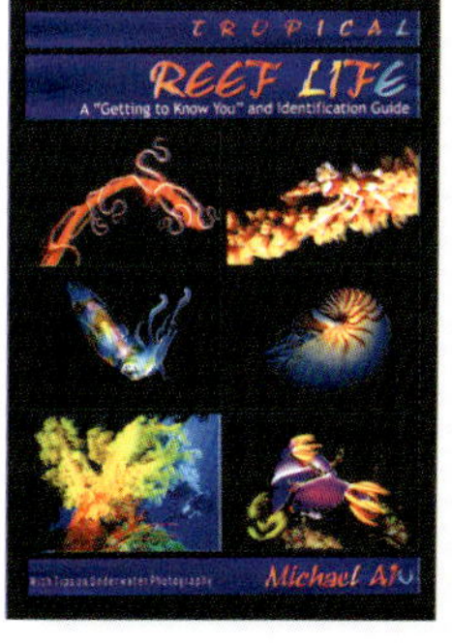

Special Autographed copies available for owner of "An Essential Guide to Digital Underwater Photography" Email: one@oneocean.com to order.

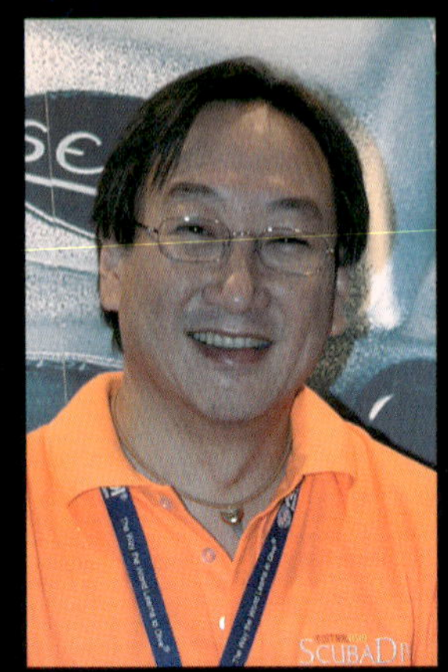

About the Authors

Michael AW: *Pursuing the art form of documentary photography, Michael AW is well known for his saturated colour imagery. His work on environmental issues and natural history, have been featured in over 100 magazines including BBC Wildlife, Asian Geographic and GEO. He has received several international awards including in the BBC Photographer of the Year Wildlife Competition. He has authored over 30 natural history books about fishes, corals, invertebrates, dive travels and he have also contributed to the Encyclopedias of Malaysia and Indonesia.*

Mathieu Meur: *Growing up in Mauritius, Mathieu developed a love for the sea at an early age. A jack-of-all-trades, he divides his time between his day job as an engineer, his weekends teaching diving and underwater photography, and the rest of the time conducting seminars and writing articles for regional dive publications. Mathieu is currently based in Singapore, which allows him to dive around the region. In 2001, Mathieu authored a PADI-approved Distinctive Speciality course entitled 'Underwater Digital Photographer.'*

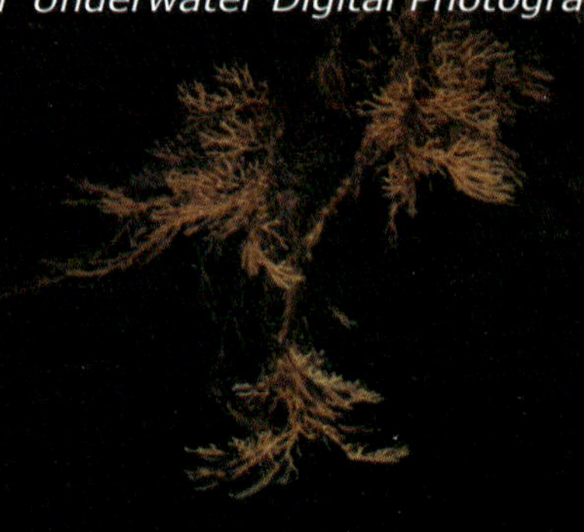

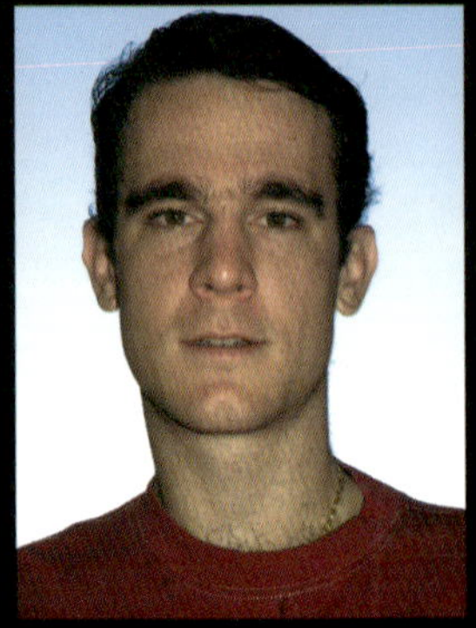